drawing and designing children's and teenage fashions

drawing and designing children's and teenage fashions

Patrick John Ireland, MSIAD

B.T. Batsford Ltd, London

Patrick John Ireland at work
in his studio.
Photograph by Kate Salway

First published 1979

Printed by The Anchor Press Ltd,
Tiptree, Essex
for the Publishers B.T. Batsford Ltd,
4 Fitzhardinge Street, London
W1H 0AH

ISBN 0 7134 1333 6

Contents

Acknowledgments

Alan Hamp of Batsford for his generous help with some of the more technical aspects of the production of the book. The staff of the library of the London College of Fashion, who were always helpful in aiding my research. Miss Patricia Wedderburn for her help on the technical terms of fashion. Miss Edith Fuller, Mr John and Mrs Ursula Wilson for the interest they have taken in my work. Samuel Carr for his encouragement and advice as editor of my books.

Introduction

This book is to help students when designing and drawing fashion garments for children and teenagers.

The first section illustrates the proportions of a child and the development of the age groups.

With the aid of the figure charts the student can relate the proportions of the child to a design.

The method of figure drawing illustrated will enable the student to develop, with practice, a number of poses on which to sketch designs according to the age group. Suggested exercises, areas of research and design projects are given in the different sections of the book.

The three main methods and techniques in drawing illustrated in the book are:

1 Design Sketching and Development sheets
2 Working or Production sketches
3 Presentation Drawings

Part two covers the designing of children's fashion and takes the student through the basic principles of design. There are individual sections on the various aspects of design.

The design briefs have been set to cover a wide variety of clothes for many different occasions. They include suggested areas of specific study.

When designing children's clothes it is important to have a general awareness of the kind of clothes that appeal to young children and teenagers, taking into account the colours, fabrics and general effects that are in vogue. It is necessary to have a feeling for fashion in the future and the influences that are creating new trends, e.g. colours, fabrics, textures and patterns, and the way in which clothes are co-ordinated and accessorised in terms of shoes, boots, socks, caps and scarves, etc.

The practical aspects of the design must be considered:

1 The age group for which you are designing, taking into account the proportions of the child within that group, and any specific figure problems in that age group.

2 The activities for which you are designing, e.g. casual wear, play garments, clothes for a specific sport, school uniforms, separates, holiday wear or party wear. Study the activities or occasions before creating ideas. Note the situation and environment in which the garment would be worn.

3 Selecting fabrics suitably related to the activity, wear and stress (general maintenance, e.g. dry cleaning, non-iron, easy care).

4 The most suitable pockets, fasteners, and style features generally related to the wearer's activities. The adaptability of certain features and the way in which they will be used must also be considered.

5 When working for a specific market the professional designer will naturally bear in mind the market – and price – in which the design would be retailed.

Sources of inspiration and research

A designer will use many different areas of research when looking for inspiration. A constant awareness of the fashion-mood and future trends is essential. This is achieved by studying the latest fashion magazines and articles in the newspapers, visiting trade exhibitions, fashion shows and generally taking note of any new influence that may affect fashion.

A designer working on a collection and looking for new ideas and sources of inspiration would use many different areas of research: the periods of historic costume, national and military uniforms, the decoration and embroidery of different countries; and design from the influences of Architecture, Painting, Films, Theatre, Ballet and Opera. The study of plant forms, flowers and nature generally produces inspiration for the existing use of form, colour, textures and patterns.

Always be aware of the possible use of new fabrics, trimming and decoration; have a folder and sketch book in which to keep and collect information for future reference.

Collect cards of paintings and objects when visiting art galleries, museums and exhibitions. Make sketches of anything you feel may be of use. These little sketches – an object, plant or particular decoration, may be used later as a starting point for a theme for a collection of garments when adapted and developed.

When using costume research as a source of inspiration for design ideas you may use and adapt only a detail from a costume: the shape of a neck line, collar or sleeve, the use of a trimming or the treatment of a particular fabric.

Fabric selection

Collect fabrics for reference when designing. Make notes on the new colours, patterns and textures. Experiment with the fabrics – relating the fabrics in different combinations.

When beginning a design development sheet it is helpful to collect your fabrics and trimmings together and develop a fabric board, relating the colours, patterns and textures and considering the volume of colour when arranging the samples. Add the trimmings, ribbons, lace, cord, etc., placing them against the samples you feel look the most attractive.

Selecting fabrics for a collection is a very important stage in the design process. A selection of fabrics is built up after careful consideration and after viewing many collections. The designer will view the collections some months before starting on a new range of fashion garments.

Story board

When working on a new collection and choosing fabrics, trimming, etc. the professional designer will usually create a story board. This is done with the help of a large screen or board on which selected sample fabrics will be displayed, comparing the colours, tones and textures and related trimmings and design sketches. This board would gradually develop as the fabrics are selected and displayed, until the fashion story or theme begins to emerge. The story board is an excellent way of developing a collection. It enables a design team to discuss the possibilities of the use of fabrics and colours related to design sketches, and eventually the 'accessorising' of a collection should a fashion show be arranged.

For a student it is good practice to make a story board on a small scale, when designing a collection, by using a piece of card on which you arrange your sample fabrics and trimmings before starting on your design development sheets. This can prove a fruitful source of inspiration for your designing.

Design development sheets

Having chosen the fabrics you intend to use for your collection the next stage will be to develop a theme on which your designs will be based. In some instances the designs are produced first and the fabrics are selected for them. One of the methods a designer uses to develop and experiment with ideas is to produce a series of sketches on a theme. Many sketches would be made in the designer's own particular style, which is often referred to as his 'handwriting'.

For a student it is helpful to develop ideas on sheets of paper, introducing front, side and back views, with sample pieces of fabric, trimmings and notes when necessary. Colour and pattern may be added to the sketches, indicating the use of the fabric suggested. It is more effective to keep to a colour scheme on the sheet as this adds a sense of continuity.

This type of sheet is helpful when the work of a student is being assessed as it gives a clear idea of how the ideas are developed and of the way in which a student works.

Working drawings

The working drawing or production sketch is a clear diagrammatic sketch of the design selected to be made. The design should be drawn in an analytical way, and should give all the necessary information for the production of the design. It is important to indicate all seams, darts and style features in detail, with grain lines showing the way in which the fabric will be cut. Sample fabrics and a list of trimmings should be added. The drawing must be in proportion to the figure to enable the pattern cutter to produce the correct effect.

As a student of design you may be expected to produce this type of drawing to accompany the design drawing for an assessment of your work, examination or competition. This type of drawing looks effective when produced in a clean line, using a sharp pointed pencil or a *Rotring* pen. The layout and general arrangement should be carefully considered.

Fashion Buyer A person who buys for a fashion department in a store or shop.

Wholesale Wholesale is selling of garments to the buyers of retail shops and stores. Wholesalers usually have showrooms where they display the garments for buyers to view. Representatives may take a new range of garments to buyers of departmental stores and other retailers.

Retail Retail is the selling of fashion garments to the consumer through stores, shops and boutiques.

Fashion illustrator Fashion illustrators produce work for magazines, newspapers, catalogues and advertising purposes generally. They are concerned with producing drawings suitable for reproduction working in line, tone and colour. The fashion illustrator must be constantly aware of the current feeling for fashion and future trends.

Toile and sample garments

When designs have been chosen from the sketches the garments will be developed further. The sample workroom would produce a toile made in a plain cotton fabric (cambric); or in some instances, if the fabric is not too expensive, a sample garment would be made in the selected fabric. This enables the designer or design team to see the garment as it is made and develop the design further, correcting the silhouette, proportion, balance and general effects. The production pattern, the pattern layout and costing would be developed at this stage before the design went into production.

When the garments are finally complete they would be sold wholesale to fashion buyers. In many instances fashion shows are staged by a manufacturer to display a new collection of garments to the buyers. The orders are made and finally the garments would be sold retail in stores, shops and boutiques.

Presentation drawings

These are made if you are selling your ideas or wish to send a collection of sketches of a current collection to buyers. The drawings would be made to a standard size. This makes it easier for the sketches to be handled and is more convenient if they are being sent by post. The presentation sketches should reflect the complete look the designer wishes to project and should include all necessary details, fabric samples and back view. In some instances colour may be added. Often the sketches would be copies and printed for presentation in a folder for fashion buyers to view.

Many designers engage a fashion illustrator or fashion sketcher to produce this type of drawing, which would be suitable for reproduction and advertising purposes.

The working drawing must be very clear – giving full information. The placement of seams, pockets and other details must be considered with care. Certain details may need to be drawn on a large scale to indicate seams and the finer points of the design.

Written information may be added when required together with a sample of the fabric.

Note in the working sketch illustrated how the details of the collar have been shown as a separate aspect.

Drawing children

When drawing children and designing for different age groups it is important to be aware of the changing proportions of the growing child.

The method illustrated will help the student to sketch the figure and work out the correct proportions related to the age.

For the beginner it is helpful to work from the charts, as illustrated, constructing the figure and using the method of the number of heads that would fit into the length of body. Note the size of the head and the length of arms, legs and feet according to age.

Work from the book, make drawings of each age group, then practise by sketching the figures from memory. This will help considerably when you begin designing for a specific age group.

If possible sketch from life, observing children's attitudes, the way in which they move, walk, skip and climb, etc. It is difficult to draw children in a set pose as they are not very patient models. It is better to make quick sketches from life and then develop them.

Illustrated throughout the book are different techniques, using pen, pencils, felt pens, paints and pastels, etc. – a variety of different methods of producing a fashion design sketch from a realistic to a more stylized drawing.

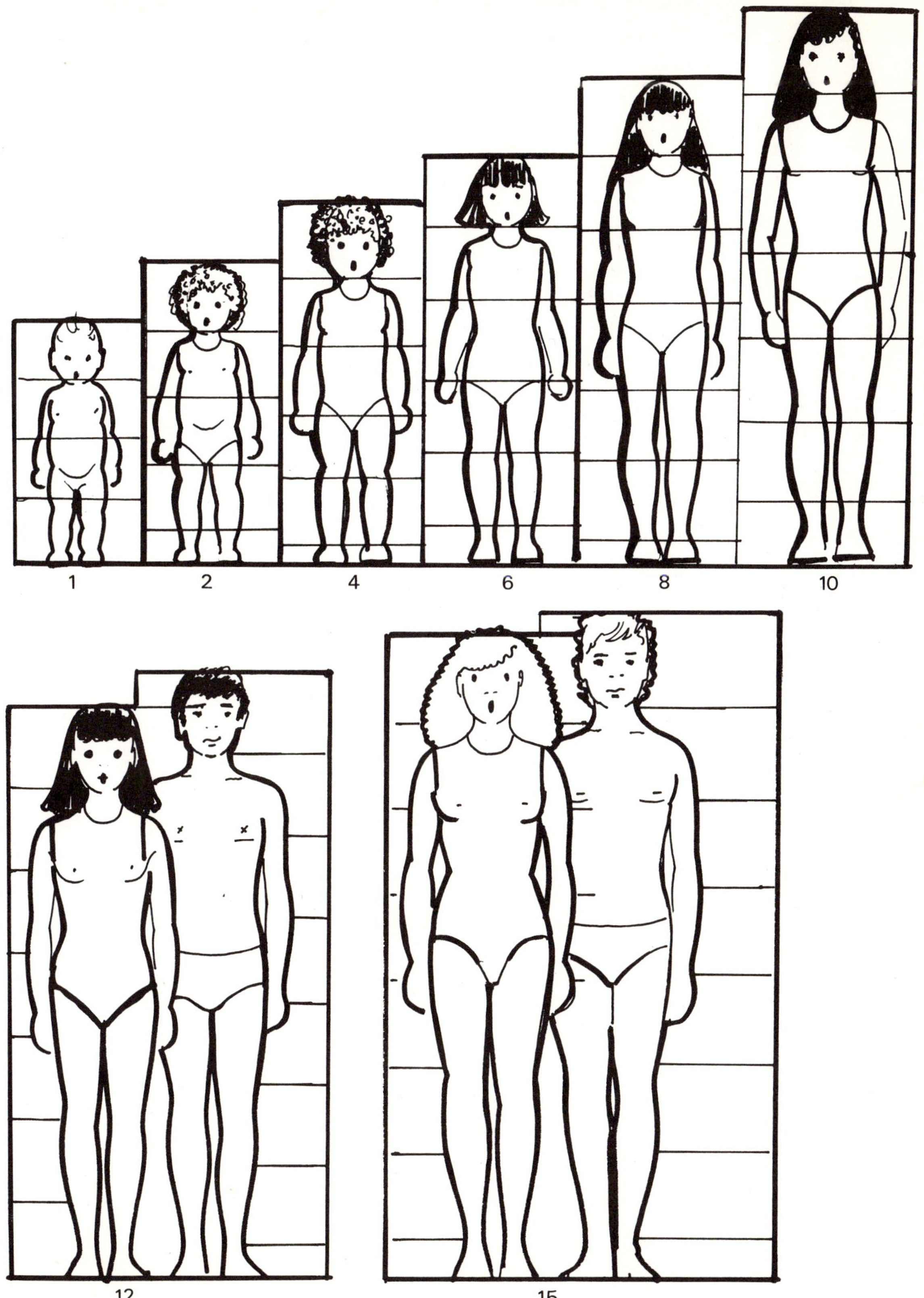
1
2
4
6
8
10
12
15

During the early stages of growth the infant's limbs are proportionately short. The upper limbs of an infant at first are longer than the lower.

The middle line of the body is above the umbilicus; after two years it is on the umbilicus; after this it is below this point.

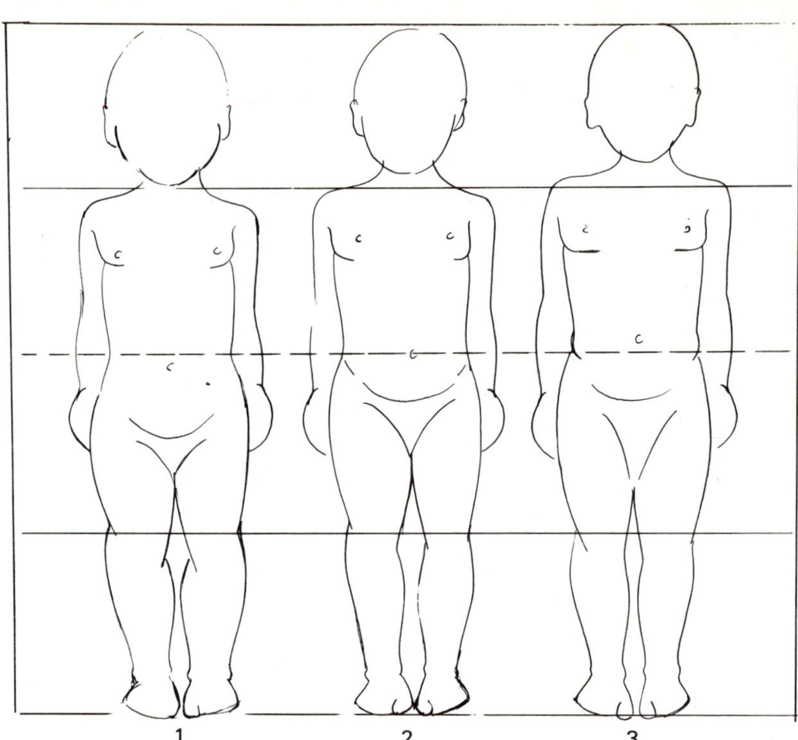

Three years
Note the stylized technique used in the presentation of the beach outfits. The proportions have been observed from the figure chart. The designs have been developed over the figures with the aid of a semi-transparent paper.

Three-four years

The construction of a figure seen from different angles. It is useful when designing and developing ideas on paper to sketch the design from various angles.

It is good practice to sketch the figure, working from the basic proportions and then to develop a number of poses, changing the positions of the arms, legs and feet, etc.

If you use semi-transparent paper you can develop the drawings further by tracing over your own sketches and making necessary corrections.

Figures illustrating a dress seen from different angles
Note the folds from the bodice and the way in which they fall giving movement to the dress.

Four-five years

When sketching you should remember that the figure proportions are based on the number of heads into the body according to the age group.

The balance line falls from the neck. This line will indicate which leg is taking the weight of the figure.

The beginner should always sketch the figure in first with very light pencil lines and check the position of waist, hips and overall proportions. When sketching the garment you will find it most helpful to draw lightly a line following the contour of the body. This will serve as a guide when designing and placing relative details.

The illustration on the opposite page was produced with a black soft pencil – for the details the pencil was sharpened to a very fine point.

Six-seven years

As a child develops, its attitudes and behaviour will change.

Observe children of different ages. Note their attitudes and movements.

Make quick sketches of them for future reference. Experiment with different hair styles and facial expressions.

As you gain more confidence you will discover new techniques of drawing.

Seven years

The length of the arm is equal to the leg to the crutch. After this the length is shorter (see illustrations).

Ten years

The foot is the same length as the head. After the age of ten the foot is longer.

The number of head-lengths in the body varies with the different age group, as illustrated.

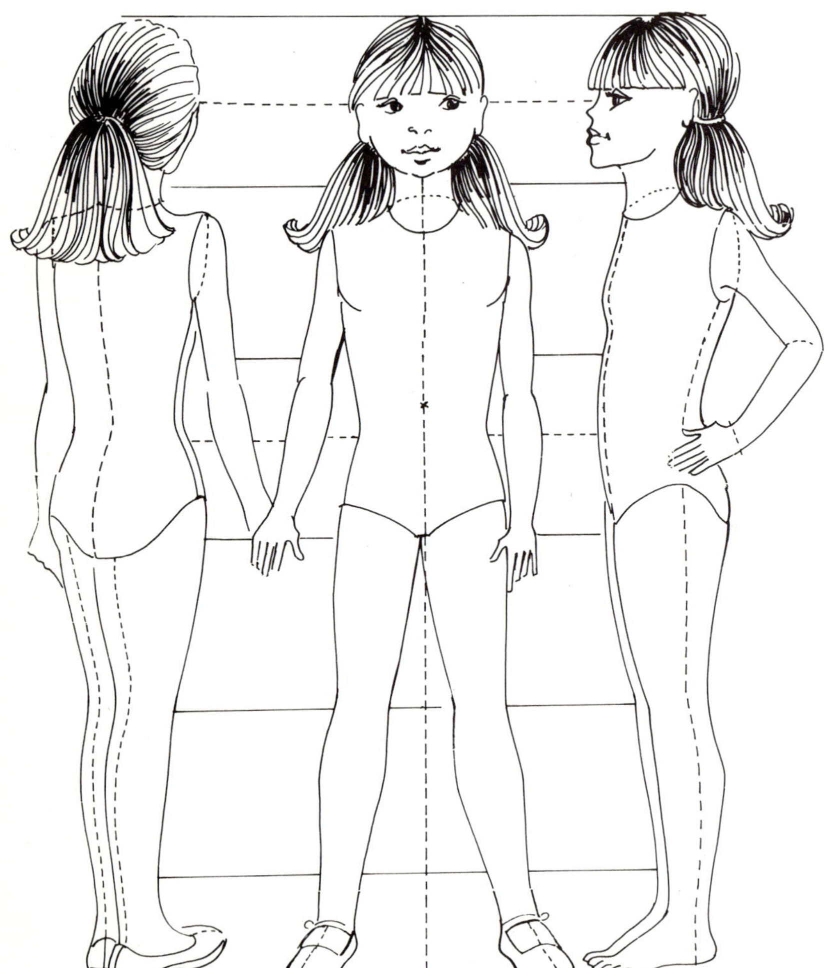

The presentation drawing on the right was produced with a Pentel propelling drawing pencil with a very fine lead, producing a sharp line value for the drawing of the hair, the draw-string tie at the waist, the gathers, and the elastication on the bodice and hem of the trousers. When drawing gathers and folds of fabric consider with care the way in which the fabric would fall.

Eight years

Observe the balance line from neck to the foot taking the weight of the figure. It is important to check this at the early stage of sketching the figure. If it is not correct the figure will not look as if it is standing.

When the legs in a pose are placed to take the weight on each leg the balance line falls in between as illustrated.

For the illustration on the right a number of different pencils were used to attain the various textures and line values.

This type of drawing would be suitable for presentation when working on a collection of designs. Note the attention given to the details of the garments, i.e. pockets, fastenings, and seam placement.

Eight years

When sketching garments on the figures remember to draw the garments round the figure. Consider the way the fabric would be cut and how it would fall, depending on the fabric.

The illustrations indicate the first quick-lines sketched round the figures. In the final drawings the folds of the skirts have changed the hem line.

Facing Page

1 As an exercise, sketch the figure, working on the principle of heads into the figure. Then develop the same figure in different poses. Sketch lightly the construction lines of the figure, then develop the garment design over the figure.

2 *The figures complete with dresses.* Details of gathers, seams, collar, etc., would be added at this stage.

Ten years

The illustration on the opposite page has been developed with H.B. (hard) and 2.B. soft pencils.

Note the concentration on the soft gathers in the skirt and sleeves of the dress and the careful attention given to the detail of the smocking on the bodice, sleeve and pockets.

A simple background has been added to give atmosphere. This type of drawing would be produced for presentation when showing a collection of designs for buyers and advertising purposes.

Fifteen, sixteen, seventeen years
From the basic pose develop a number of poses which will enable you to sketch your designs from different angles.

Experiment with new hair styles as the fashion changes. A few lines will suggest a style without going into too much detail.

Select the pose most suitable for the design, considering the type of garments, e.g. whether casual, elegant, sporty, etc.

Two stages of design sketching

1 Rough out the figure pose with a free line. The poses need only be suggested with a light pencil line.

2 Sketches developed with the designs sketched over the figures. Note the different poses showing the dress from a variety of angles.

Right A presentation drawing of the same dress worn by three different age groups. The fabric pattern has been suggested on the left side of the figures, giving the effect of the light falling from the right.

Fibre pointed pens of different sizes were used to obtain the effects illustrated. Note the circle in the background to bring the composition together and complete the presentation.

Eighteen years

This sketch gives the average proportions of the female figure. It helps to calculate the height of the figure by the number of heads in the body.

In the average figure at eighteen and over the head will divide into the height about 7½ to 8 times.

For fashion drawing the number may be increased to 8-8½ times.

Practise developing textures of fabrics. Experiment with different media, eg. pen and ink, paints, pastels, fibre pointed pens, coloured pencils and the wide range of felt pens offering a large range of colours. The illustration on the left of two teenage figures was drawn with a Rotring drawing pen on a smooth white card. This technique is very effective when a drawing is to be photo-copied or printed and reduced in size, as the line value of the drawing remains sharp and clear.

Note the centre front line and balance line (or centre of gravity line) which drops from the pit of the neck down to the foot supporting the weight of the figure.

When suggesting the pattern of the fabric on a design it is not necessary to produce the complete pattern on the sketch — an indication is enough. Note the way in which the pattern has been introduced on the left side of the figure, giving the effect of light coming from the right.

These sketches were produced in pen and ink with a grey water colour wash. Experiment with the effect of a pattern before working directly onto your sketch. Remember to take the pattern down to scale in proportion to the figure.

Drawing faces and hair styles

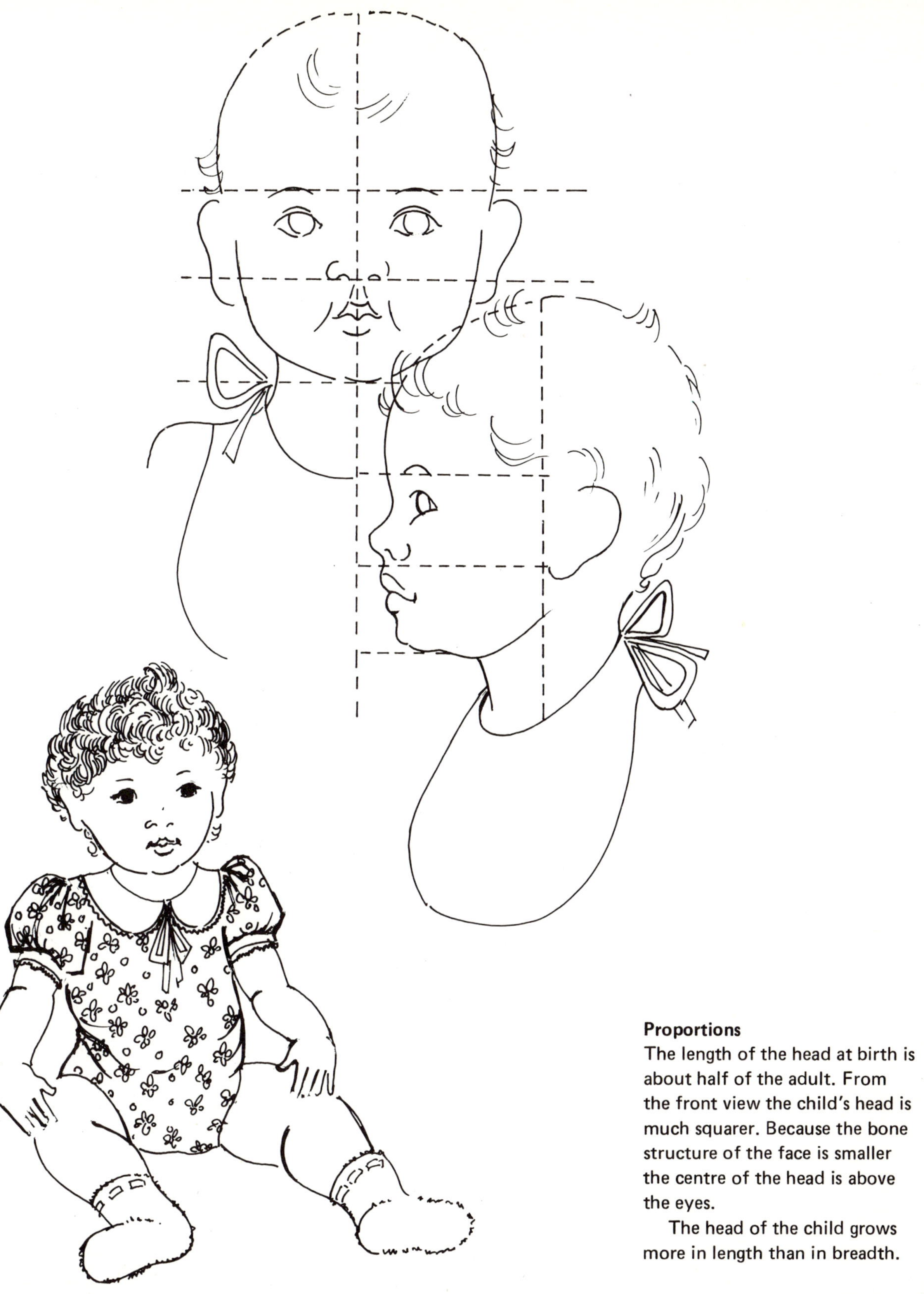

Proportions

The length of the head at birth is about half of the adult. From the front view the child's head is much squarer. Because the bone structure of the face is smaller the centre of the head is above the eyes.

The head of the child grows more in length than in breadth.

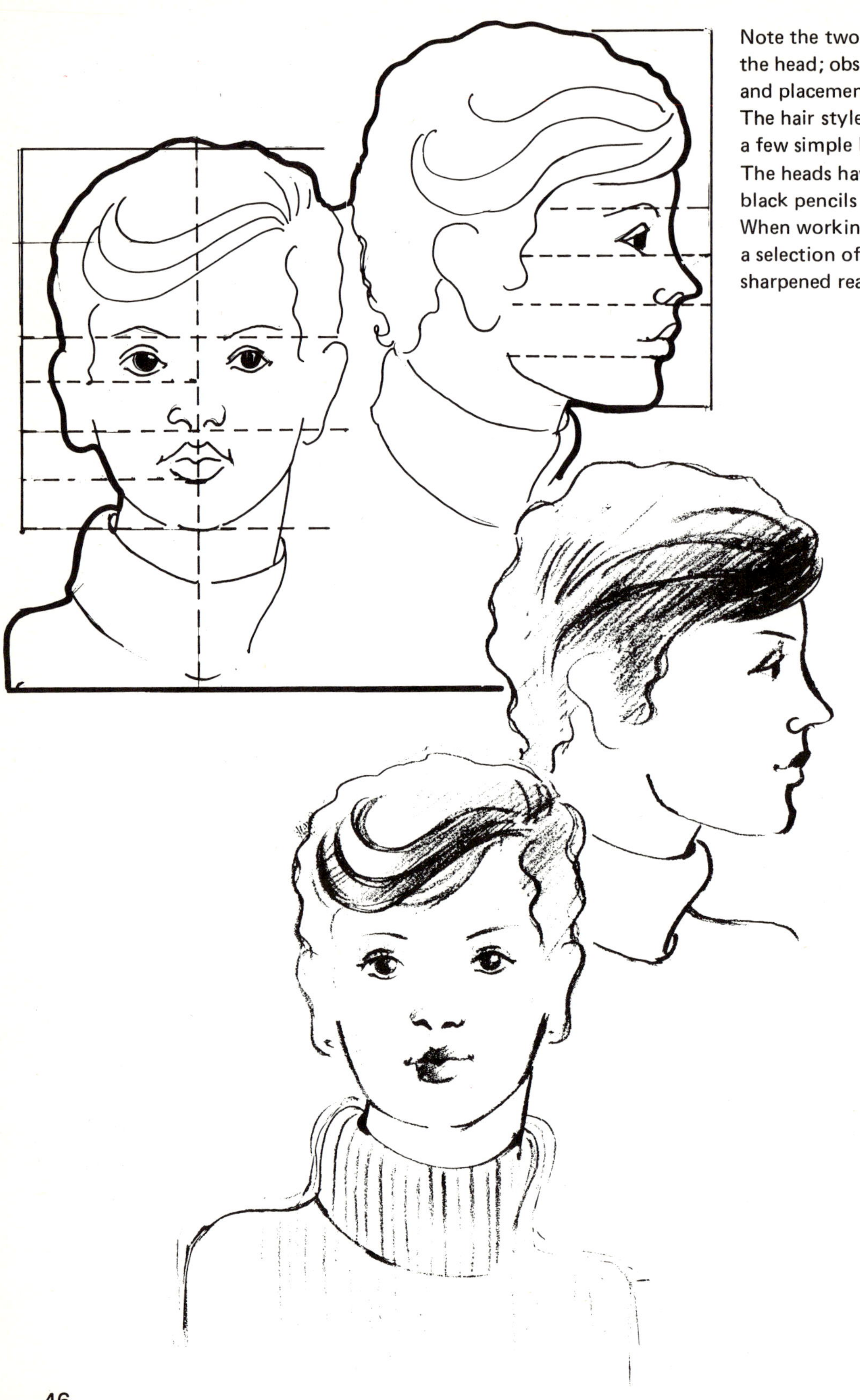

Note the two stages in drawing the head; observe the proportions and placement of the features. The hair style is suggested with a few simple lines.
The heads have been drawn with black pencils on a textured paper. When working it is helpful to have a selection of different pencils sharpened ready for use.

Note the proportions of the head. The face of the head becomes narrower as the child grows. The eyes now appear smaller as the face grows larger. Work from photographs of children; sketch from life if you are able to find a model who will sit still. Experiment with different techniques and make stylized sketches of different expressions.

In the illustration on the right the drawing methods incorporate a number of different pens and pencils to attain the various textures and line values. Rotring pen for the fine details; fibre pointed pen for stronger line values; grey magic marker for tone effects; black water colour for the hair.

The basic principles of design

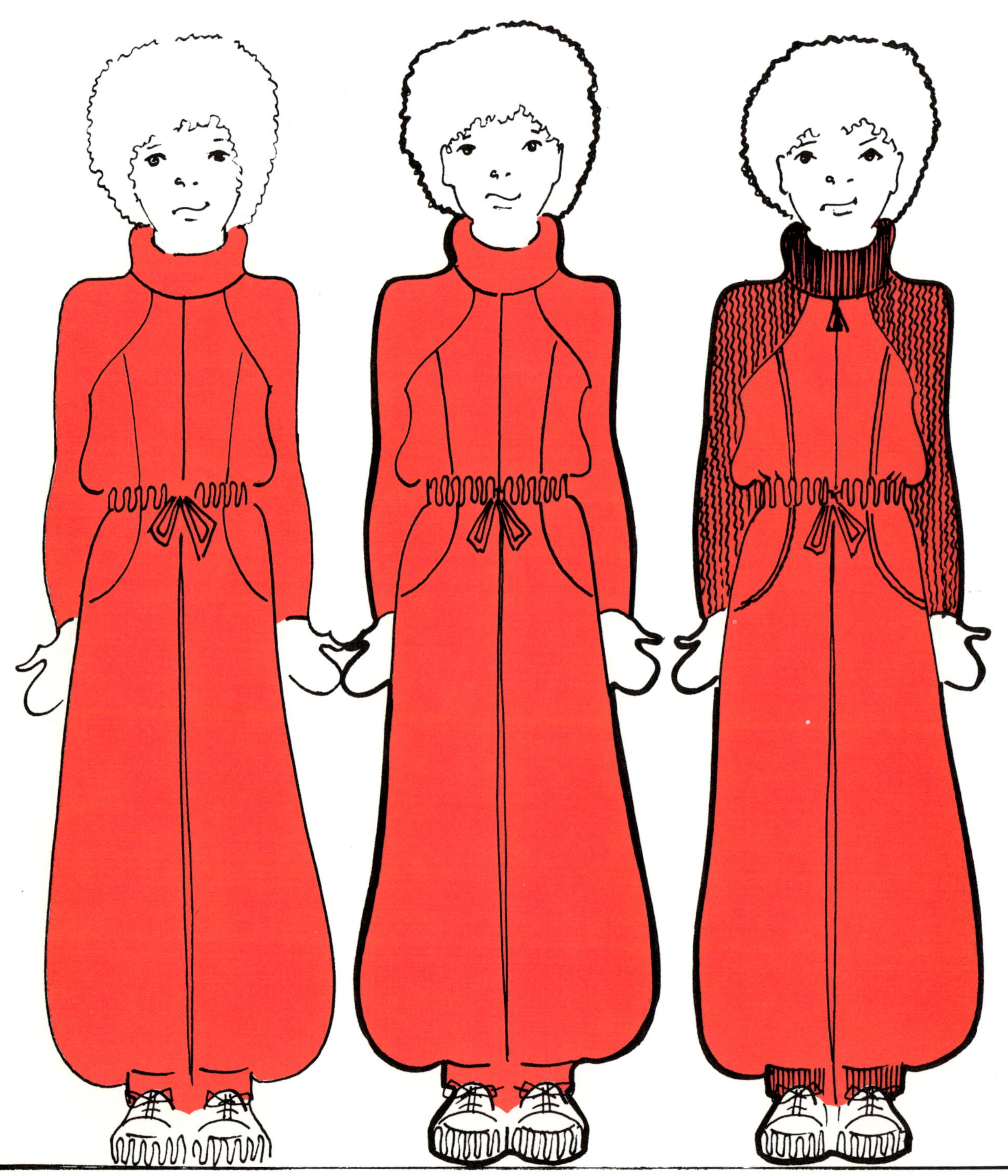

The first things to be observed at a viewing of a garment would be the colour and shape, and then the design features.

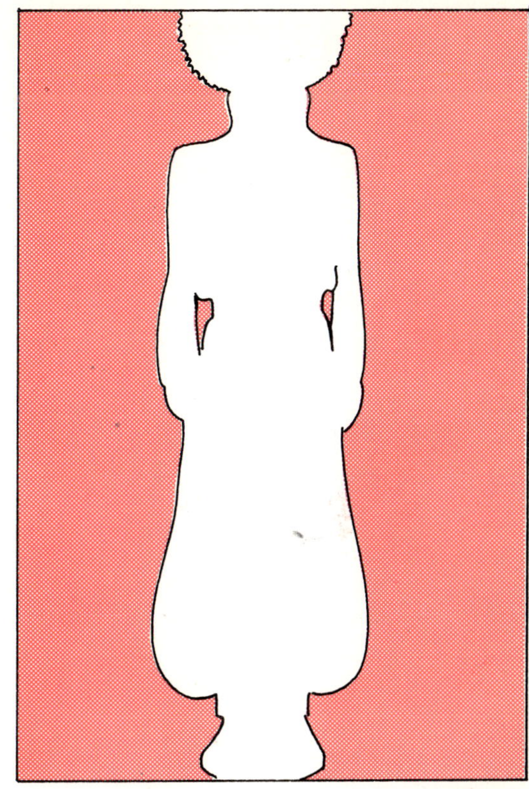

Silhouette

The silhouette is the shape or outline of any garment that is created by the designer. This is achieved through skill in cutting the pattern and through the weight and texture of the fabric. The colour, pattern and contrast or tonal effects will give different visual impressions of the silhouette. (See illustration on page 53.) Other effects are achieved with the aid of padding, linings and undergarments.

Illustrated on the following pages are examples of a few of the possibilities of changing the silhouette with the aid of pleats, gathers, frills, blousing, cutting on the bias and the raising, lowering and widening or narrowing of skirts, sleeves, neck lines, jackets and trousers.

Line The line related to fashion design is used in various ways to achieve a desired effect. A design is a combination of lines and shapes. When working on an idea the line is used to develop:

a) The silhouette
b) The style lines within the silhouette
c) The details
d) To create illusions, particularly when designing to conceal or to emphasize certain proportions.

1 Trace one figure a number of times and develop a variety of silhouettes, and the use of line and contrasting shapes.
2 Create more shapes and introduce the effects of lines and detail within a design.

Exercise For the beginner, when working on an idea, it will prove good practice to develop one basic design many times, as illustrated.

Should you find drawing difficult at this stage, trace over one basic shape as shown.

Experiment with line, colours, textures and pattern within the one silhouette. By doing this it will be discovered that there are many design possibilities.

1 Sketch your basic figure shape using the proportions illustrated.
2 Place layout paper over the basic figure shape and work out the design.
3 Complete the design adding the details.

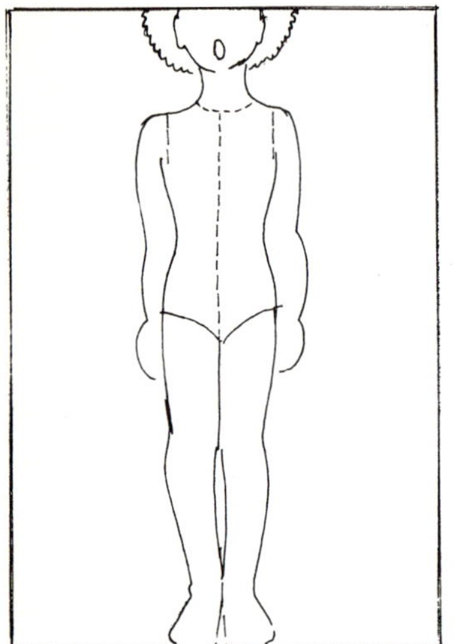

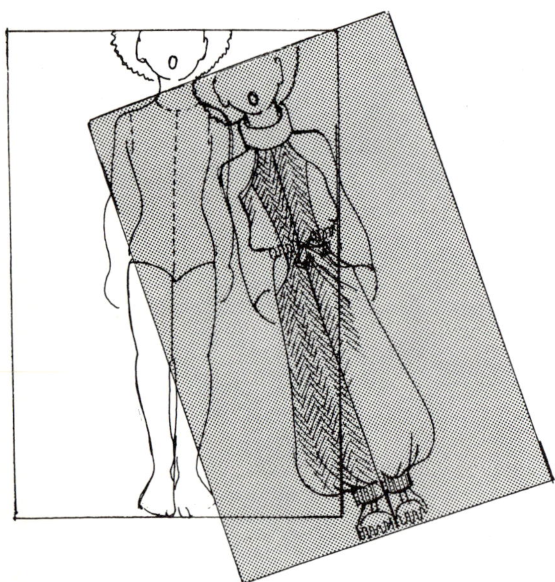

Contrast of pattern, colour and texture

Experiment with fabrics, arranging sample pieces together and relating the many effects achieved. When creating ideas it is good practice to develop the same design, introducing different colours, patterns and textures. Note how the same basic design changes with the variations in the use of fabrics.

Note the use of line introducing the horizontal, vertical, diagonal and curve.

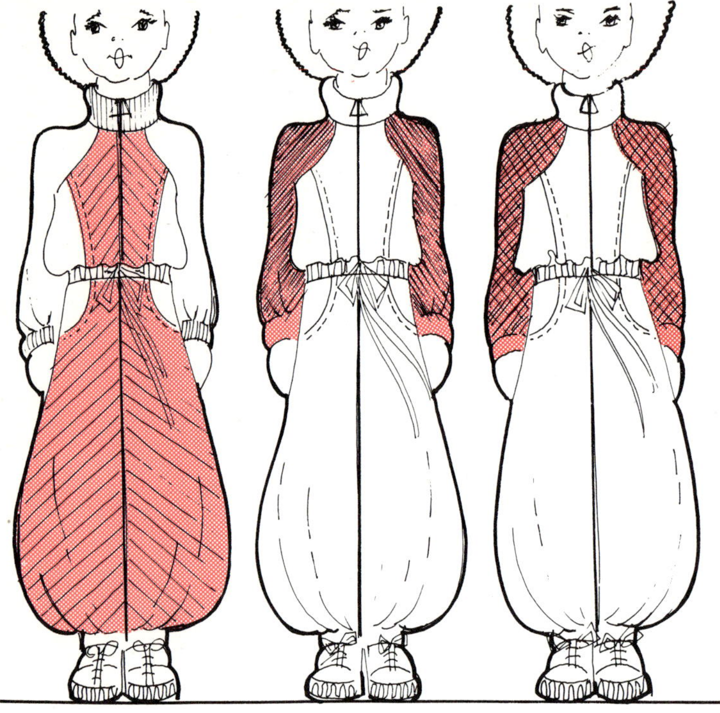

Contrasting textures

The use of fabrics and textures creates many interesting design ideas: the contrasts of leather and tweeds or fur and silk, wool, mohair and soft leather trimmings, etc., lead to many exciting effects.

As a designer you should experiment with new fabrics and textures. It is a good idea to collect sample pieces of contrasting textures. The samples need only be of small size. You will be able to refer to your collection as a source of inspiration when designing.

Design exercise

Design a summer dress for a 10 to 12 year age group. Trace the design six times or sketch the pose freehand. Select a coloured pencil or felt pen and indicate a striped patterned fabric combined with a plain fabric. Experiment with the many different effects which may be achieved with the use of stripes. Line the figures up as illustrated. Consider the overall effects and which one of the designs you consider to be the most successful.

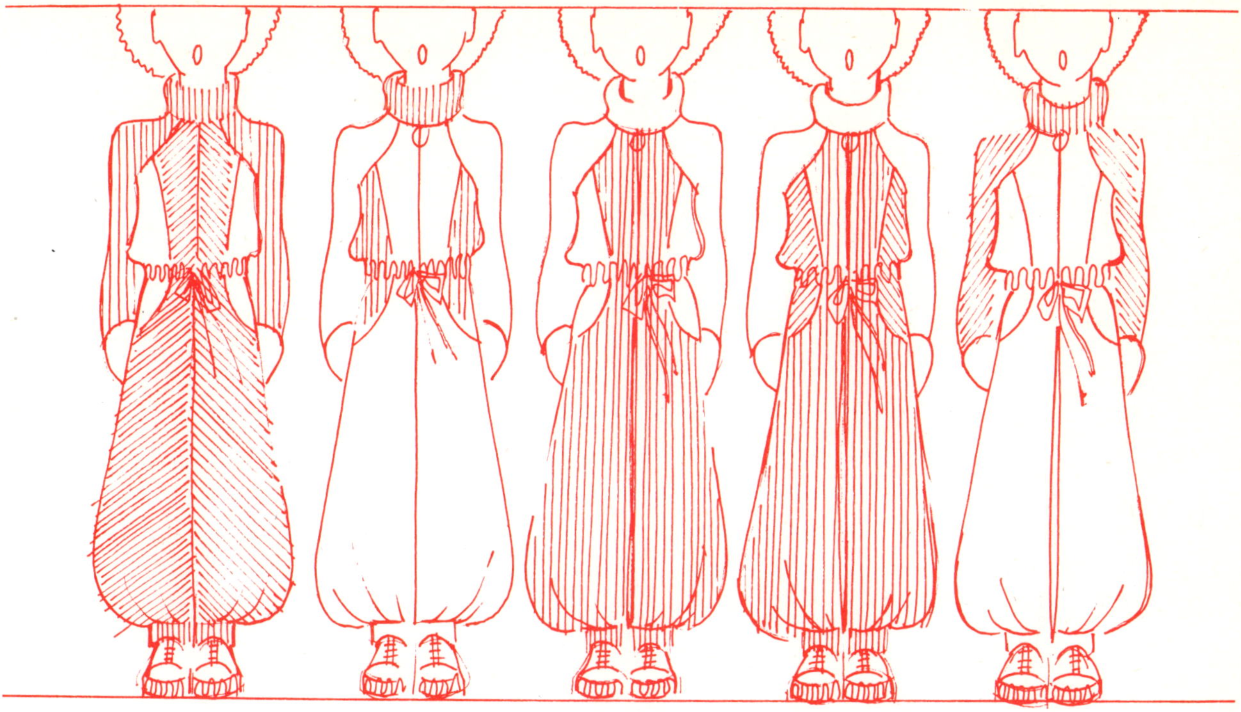

Proportion and balance

Note the way in which a different effect may be achieved with the same basic design, changing the balance and proportion of the skirt related to the bodice.

Proportion

The proportion between each line detail of a design and the whole shape or silhouette. The bodice related to the skirt or pocket in relationship to the belt, buckle and buttons.

Symmetrical balance is achieved when two masses of equal size and volume are placed at equal and opposite distances.

Asymmetrical balance is achieved when line and detail are visually balanced but are not identical.

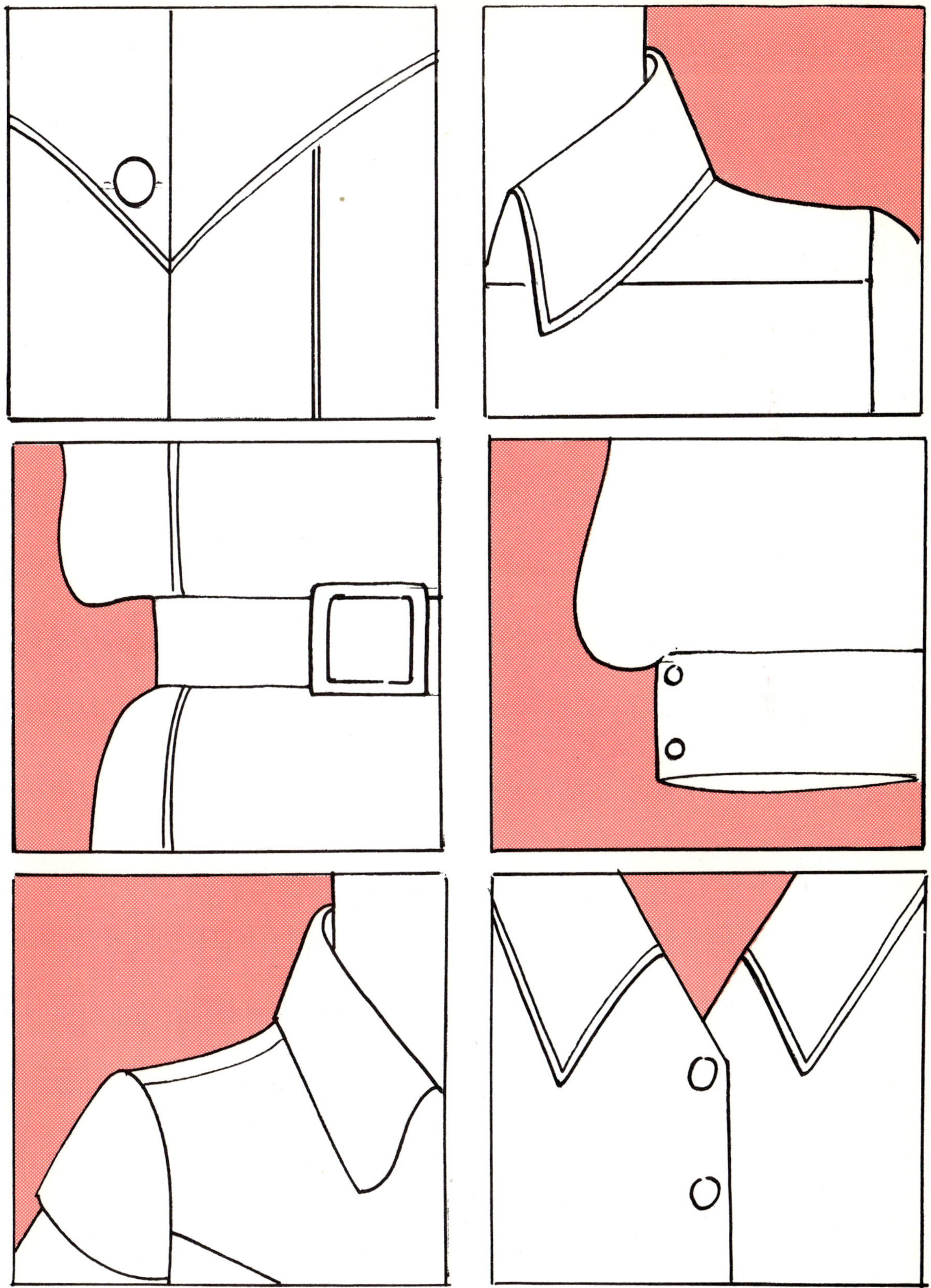

Design brief

Boys' casual summer sports shirts.
Design a collection of six sports shirts suitable for a summer holiday.
Age group: 5 to 12 years.
Collect small samples of fabric suitable for hot weather conditions.
Select plain and check fabrics to be co-ordinated. Introduce yokes as a feature of the designs.

Experiment with sample fabrics relating to the textures and patterns. As an exercise sketch one design a number of times and suggest different textures for it, noting the many effects which may be obtained with the one design.

Note the use here of herringbone, tweed and imitation lambswool combined together in casual trouser garments.

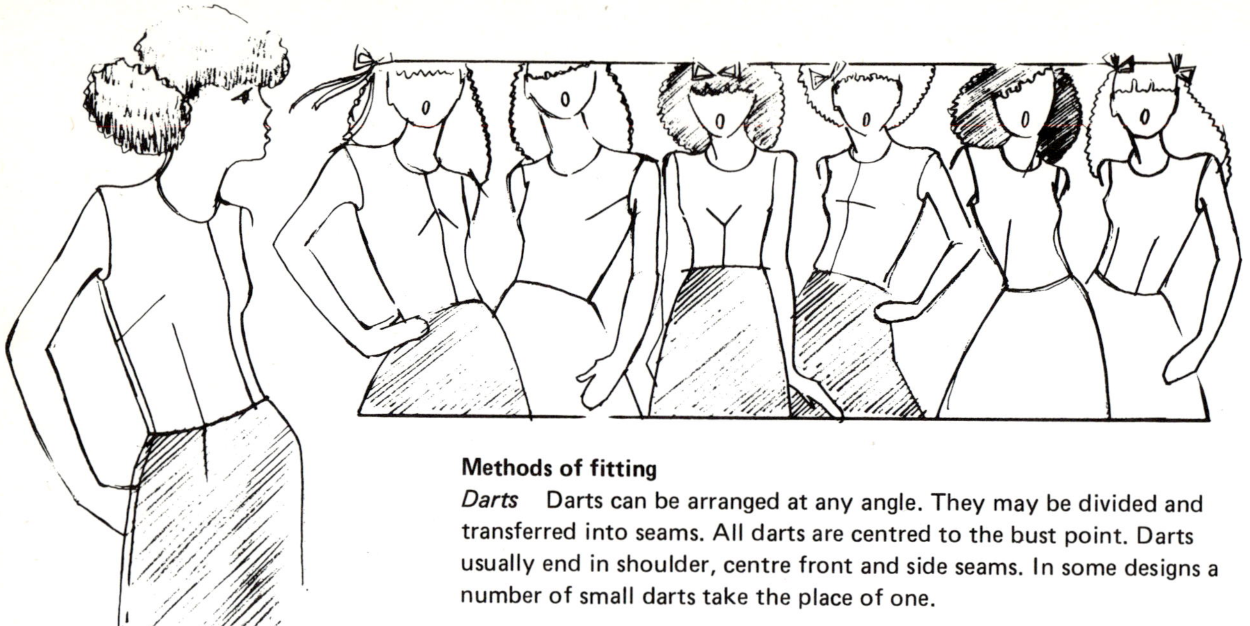

Methods of fitting

Darts Darts can be arranged at any angle. They may be divided and transferred into seams. All darts are centred to the bust point. Darts usually end in shoulder, centre front and side seams. In some designs a number of small darts take the place of one.

Seams Fitting may be incorporated in the seams and style lines of a garment.

Yokes The yoke is used for fitting, creating a neat fit to the bodice and skirt.

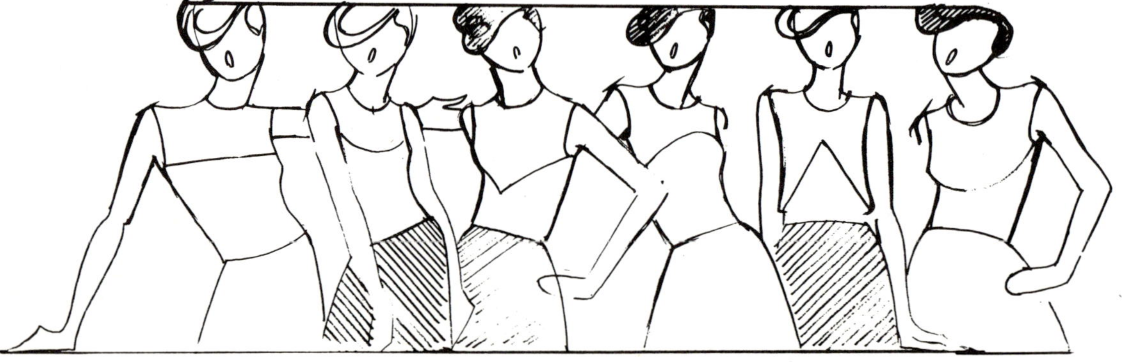

Tucks The tuck is a fold of fabric used as a decorative feature, holding fullness and used for shaping.

They may be used in many different ways in a design: on cuffs, pockets and sleeves, within yoke shapes, on the bodice, skirt, or hem. Pin-tucks are of a very narrow width and are used on yokes, cuffs, pockets, etc. Graduated tucks are arranged in a series of widths of which each one is smaller than its predecessor. Tucks in groups or spaced continuously are often used for decorative effects.

Gathers These are used for decorative effects mainly when designing in soft fabrics. Gathers are also used to control fullness and fit. They are often incorporated into bodice, sleeve, waist and skirt. The fabric will control the effects from full and deep soft gathers to the more crisp and sharp effects of a firmer fabric.

Experiment with lengths of different fabrics on a dress stand, pinning and gathering the fabric lengths. Note with patterned fabric how the gathers break into the design, giving many attractive effects.

Sleeves

From three basic styles the following design variations are made, introducing long, three-quarter, and short styles: the sleeve may be cut very full or tight; and the fabric, if patterned, may be cut on the bias to achieve certain effects; or surface decoration may be applied.

Experiment with ideas when sketching; make observations and notes in your sketch book whenever you see an unusual style. Note the way in which sleeves are cut. As you learn the techniques of pattern-cutting, you will discover different methods of adapting styles to develop new design ideas.

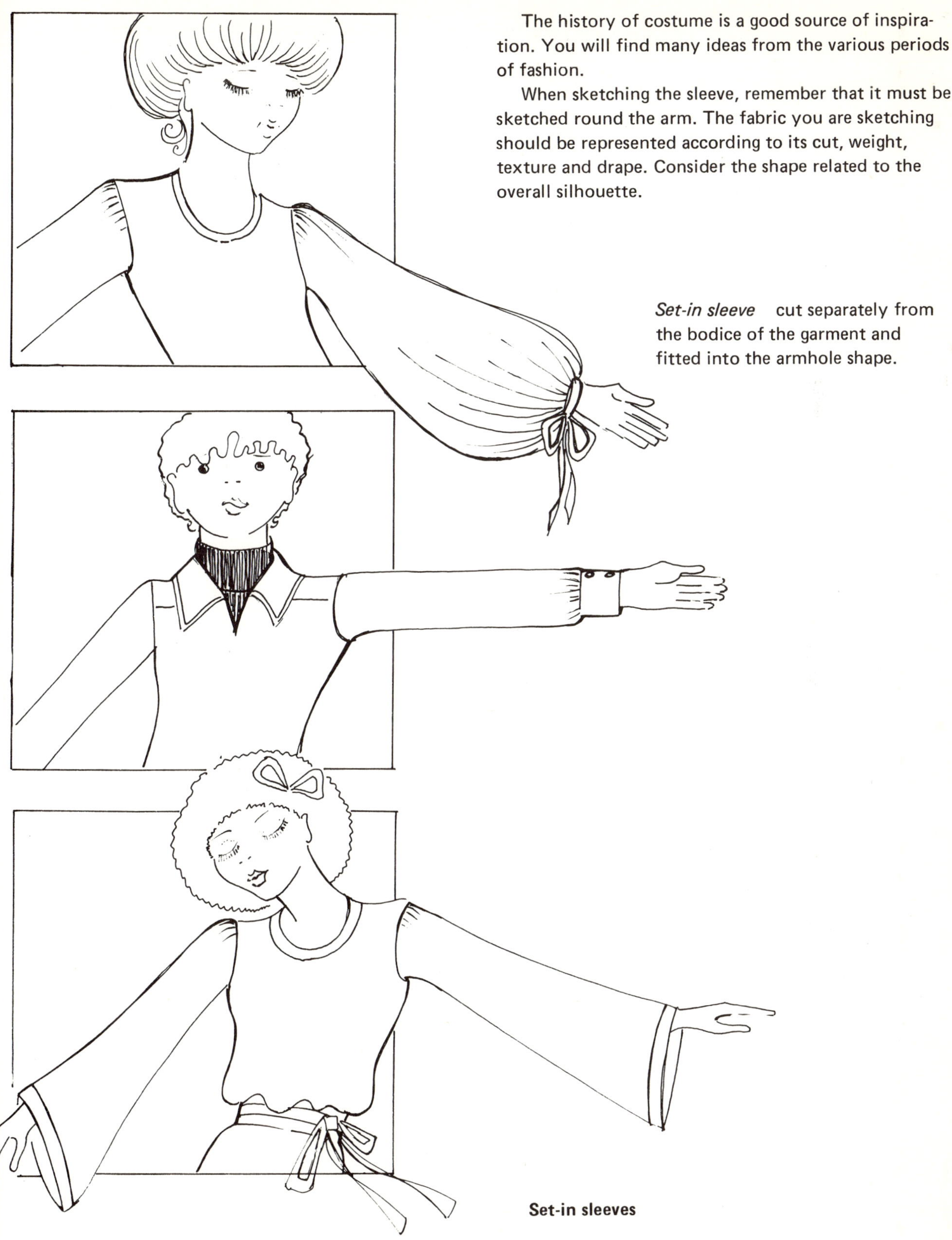

The history of costume is a good source of inspiration. You will find many ideas from the various periods of fashion.

When sketching the sleeve, remember that it must be sketched round the arm. The fabric you are sketching should be represented according to its cut, weight, texture and drape. Consider the shape related to the overall silhouette.

Set-in sleeve cut separately from the bodice of the garment and fitted into the armhole shape.

Set-in sleeves

Kimono cut in one with the body of the garment as in a Japanese Kimono.

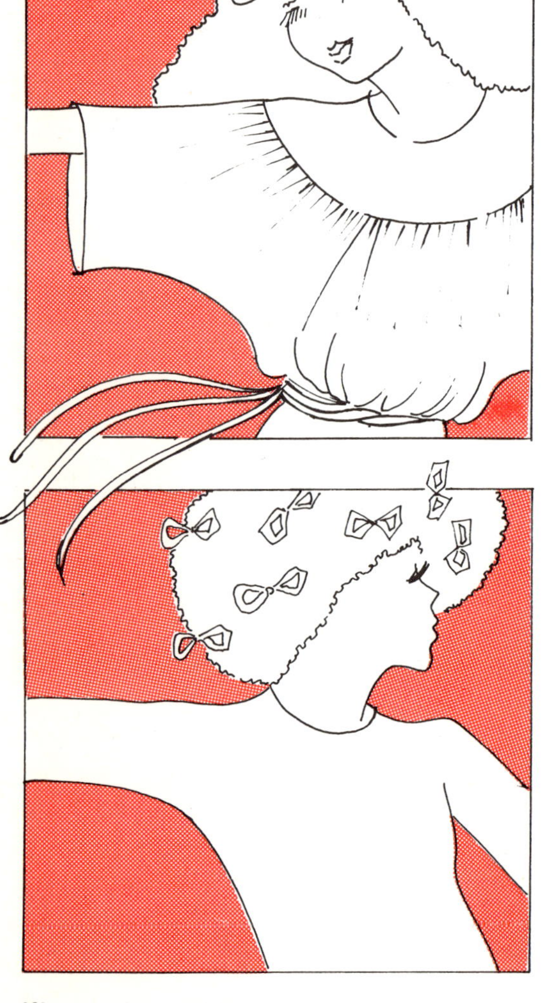

Kimono sleeve with variations

Raglan extends to the neckline and has slanting seamlines from underarm to neck in front and back.

Raglan sleeve

Extended drop shoulders

1 Full sleeve taken from panel line from the front to the back of the bodice

2 Set-in sleeve with fullness at wrist, with layers of gathered frills

3 Plain and patterned fabrics used in a kimono-cut sleeve

4 Set-in sleeves drawn in with a band of ribbon

Two designs introducing armhole shapes as a design feature.

Knitting has become a fashion feature: combined with fabric, leather and fur etc., or for a whole garment. Many pleasing effects may be achieved with the wide range of yarns of different colours, textures and weights. The patterns are varied and garments are hand-knitted or machine-knitted.

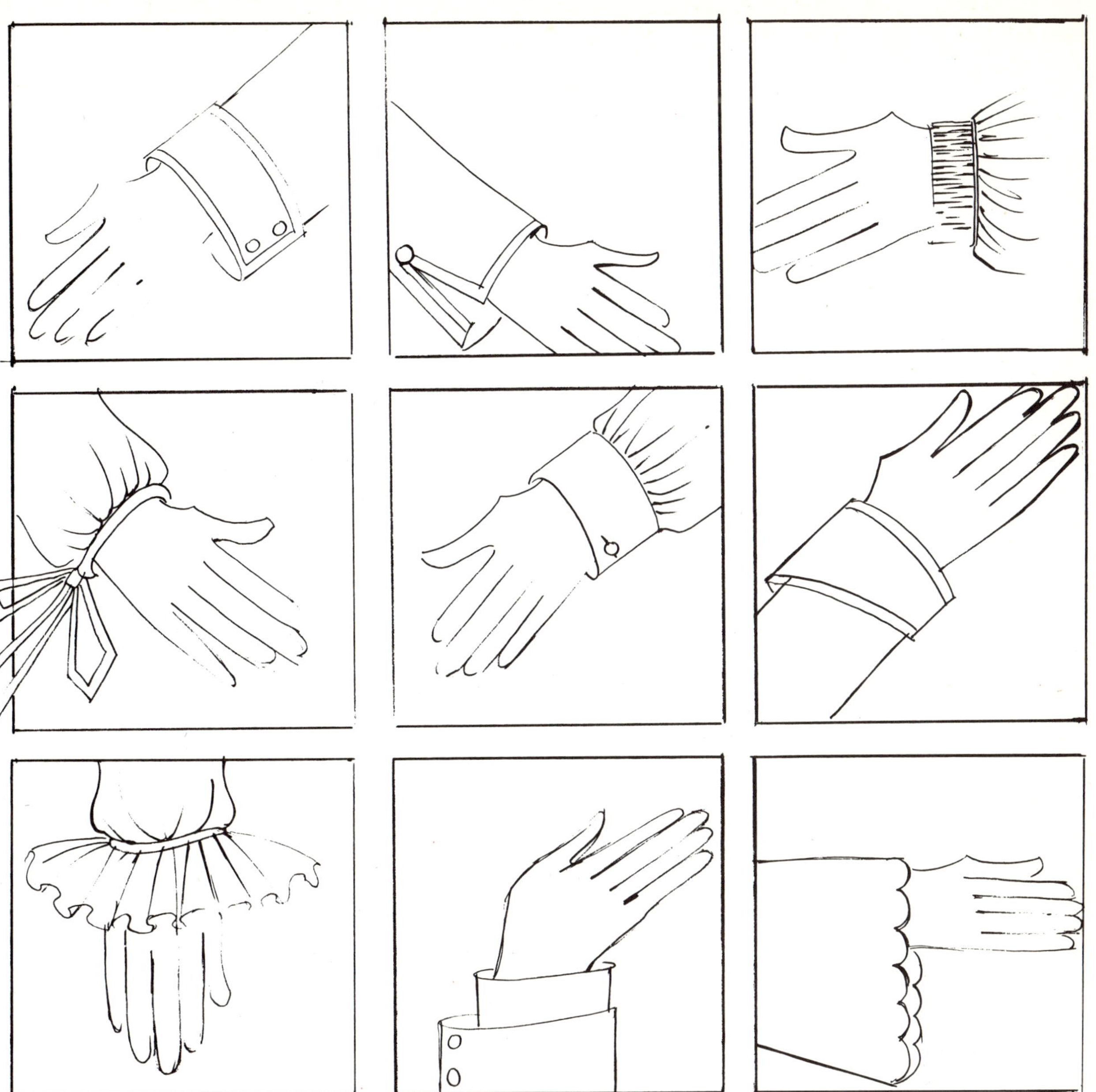

Sleeve interest added at the hem of the sleeve. A selection of design ideas have been illustrated using different effects.

Observe the many different ways of decorating the hem of a sleeve, using cuffs, frills, gathers drawn into a band, and fastenings with draw-string ties, buttons, zips and cuff links.

Develop ideas in your sketch book which you may refer to when designing. Keep a collection of fashion cuttings in your folder showing any particular details of interest.

The collar

The collar is an important feature of a garment. The designs are based on three styles from which a designer will create many variations of shape.

Apart from being a decorative feature, the collar may also serve as a practical part of a design to protect its wearer from the elements.

The three basic styles are the stand, flat and roll. The shape, when made, will vary depending on the thickness and texture of the fabric.

The proportions of the collar are important to the design of the garment related to the other features such as pockets, yokes, etc., and the whole silhouette.

A number of different styles have been illustrated through the book.

Stand The collar band standing upright from the neckline providing the height.

Fall When the collar attached to the neck band is folded back.

Style line The design or shape of the outer edge of a collar.

Break line Separates the stand and the part of the collar which turns over. The line which runs from the collar to the opening.

Neck Edge line The neck edge or neck line of the collar will influence the roll. If the collar is the same shape as the neck line of the garment the collar will lie flat; if it should be less curved at the neck edge the collar will roll and create its stand.

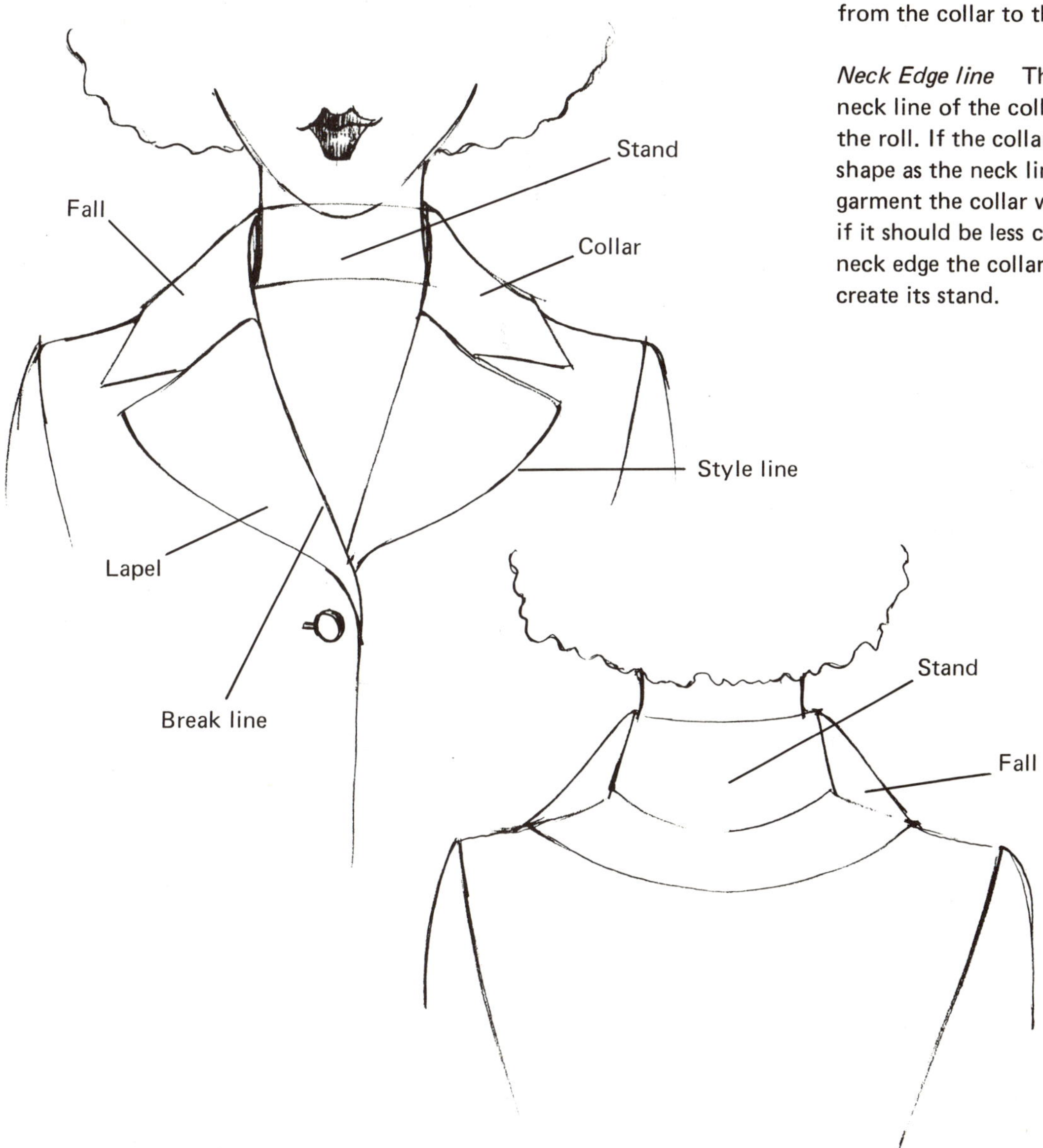

Shawl collar

The shawl collar is usually designed to wrap over in front and is held with a tie belt rather than buttons. It often figures in the designs of bath robes, dressing gowns or wrap-over coats generally.

The upper collar and lapels are cut in one piece and the collar has a roll. The collar shape may vary.

Collar with stand

This type of collar is used mainly on shirts. The collar has very little roll, it turns down at the top of the stand and is usually designed with a front opening.

Detachable collar

This collar may be designed in two ways:

1 To be worn on top of an existing collar to provide a decorative effect.

2 To be worn with a top collarless garment.

Rolled collars
This term is used for any moulded collar with curved or angled corners and a pronounced roll around the neck.

Flat collars
Many variations may be designed based on the flat collar in one or two pieces, with or without a front or back opening. The deeper the curve on the collar neck edge the flatter the collar will lie.

Stand collars
A collar known generally as the 'Mandarin' or 'band' collar.

It is a very attractive style with many variations. It can be designed to fit close to the neck, as on military uniforms, or standing away from the neck. The openings may be centre front, to the side or made at the back. The depth of the collar may vary according to the design.

Turtle neck collar (or bias turnover collar)

This collar is sometimes called a rolled collar. The correct name is Turtle neck.

It is constructed as a one-piece standing collar folded or rolled over to cover the neck seam. This collar, when worn high round the neck without rolling back, is referred to as a funnel collar.

The styles vary from deep or narrow-cut close to the neck or cut away as illustrated.

Selection of collars. Illustrated in a variety of different styles.

Consider how the neck line contributes to the silhouette of a garment.

Make a number of sketches in your sketch book, developing neck line shapes, for future reference when designing.

A selection of neck line shapes based on the use of the line from horizontal, vertical, diagonal and the curve.

Pleats

Pleats may be used within the design of a garment on the bodice, sleeve or skirt. The pleats may vary in character from soft, rolled, unpressed pleats to the very crisp, sharp knife, box and accordian pleats.

Pleats help to create the silhouette and provide controlled fullness in different parts of a garment design.

There are many variations of a number of basic styles.

The pleat is a fold in the fabric made by doubling the fabric over on itself.

Illustrated are the basic styles:

Box, Inverted, Knife and Unpressed Pleats, Accordian or Sunray Pleats – are produced by pleating companies. The styles will vary according to the cut, depth, placement and the fabric in which they are made. The fabric will provide different effects when pleated. The pattern will also create many different effects.

Exercise If you are able to sew, it is a good idea to experiment with sample pieces of fabric and with pleating, creating new effects. These you may use within your design. This can also be a way of creating ideas for a design using patterned and plain fabrics, noting the changing effects of the fabric when pleated and gathered.

Design project

Make a design sheet of party dresses suitable for an age group of between 16 – 18 years. The dresses should reflect a pretty romantic image. Use as your source of inspiration research from the Victorian period of fashion. Note the use of pleats on blouses, bodices, skirts and sleeves.

Research and Sources of Inspiration

Study books on the history of costume, old photographs, prints, costume exhibitions. Make sketches of clothes and details from garments when visiting costume museums. If you are able to sew, experiment with sample lengths of fabric with different types of pleating; observe the behaviour of the fabric and the effects of the pattern or texture when pleated.

1 Accordion pleats are straight and narrow. They resemble the creased folds in the bellows of an accordion.

2 Box pleats are a combination of two flat folds in opposite directions.

3 Inverted pleats are the reverse of box pleats. The edges meet on the outside of the garment. This pleat may be placed within a seam.

4 Knife pleats are narrow folds turned to one side.

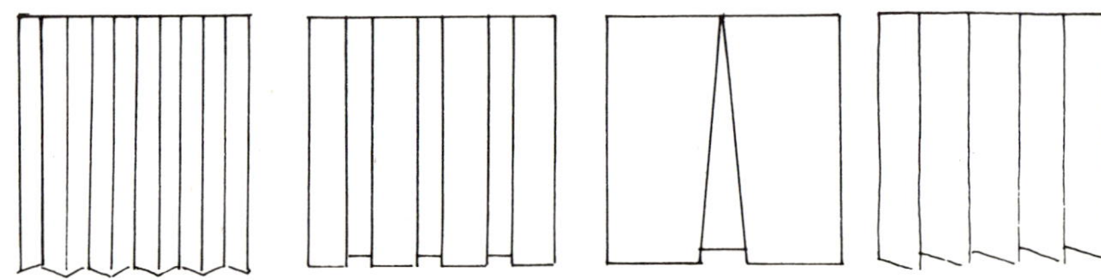

Sunray are accordian pleats that are narrow at the top and wider at the bottom. The fabric is pleated on the bias. The pleats radiate from a centre point producing a flare.

Unpressed pleats are soft pleats with edges rounded and left unpressed.

Simulated pleats are lines pressed or stitched to imitate the line of a pleat.

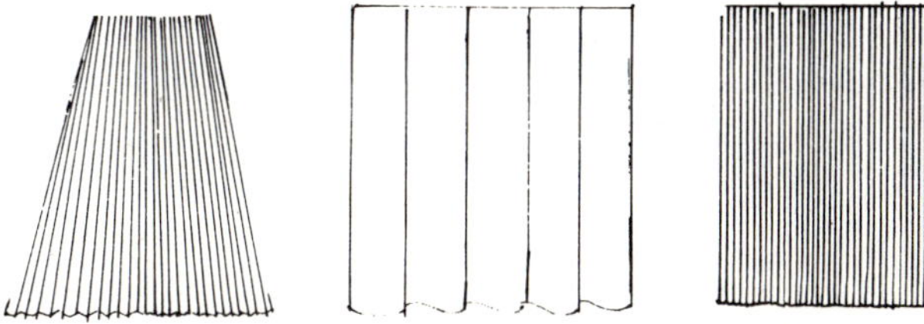

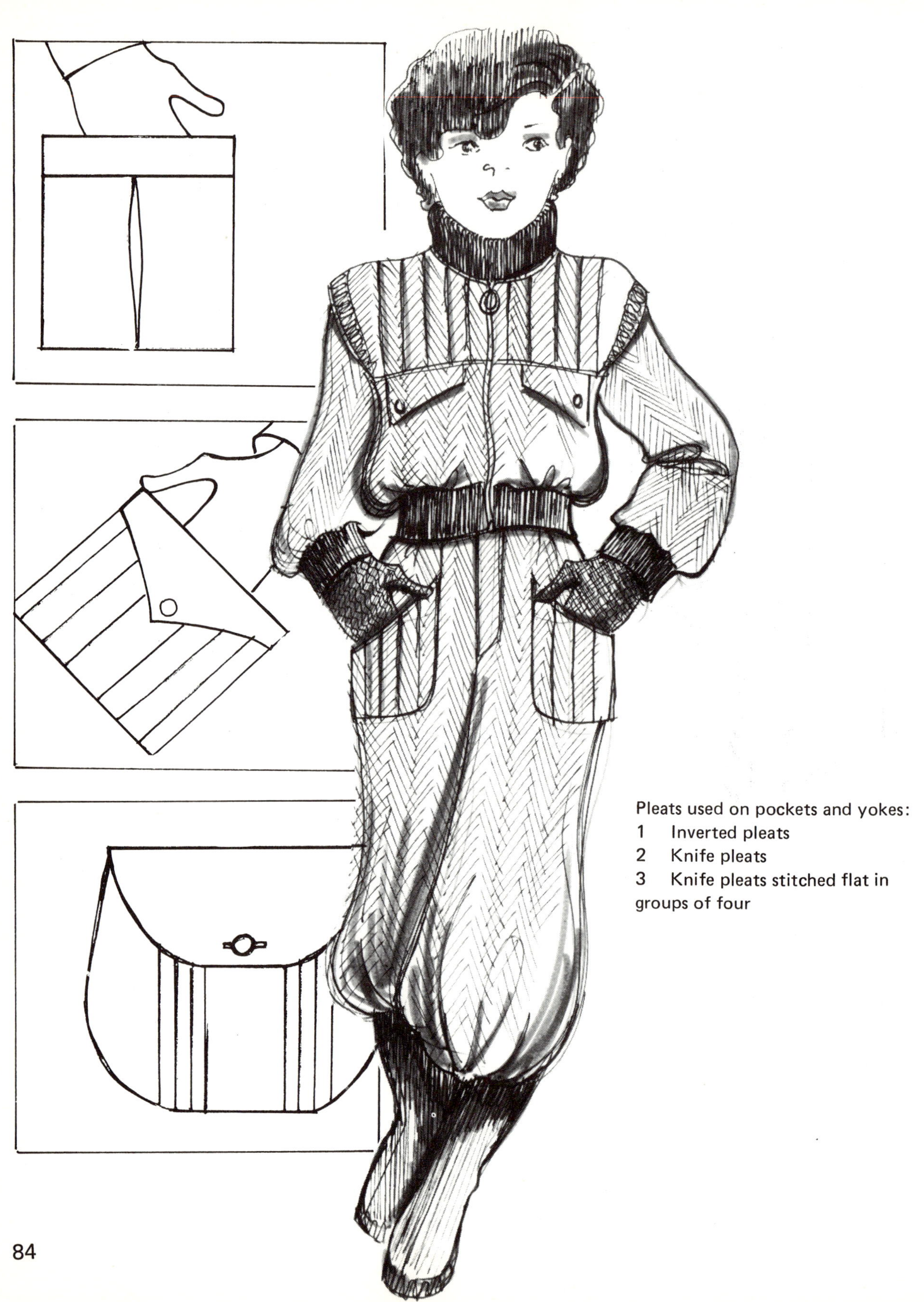

Pleats used on pockets and yokes:
1 Inverted pleats
2 Knife pleats
3 Knife pleats stitched flat in groups of four

Examples of pleats used in a design to give a decorative effect and also providing control and fit to a garment:

1 Knife pleats
2 Accordion pleats
3 Inverted pleats

1 The Godet is used to add flare to the swing of a skirt or detail on the hem of a sleeve or peplum of a dress or jacket. It can be produced by inserting a semi-circular, rectangular or pleated piece of fabric set into a seam, slash or the hem of a garment.

Peplum is a flared extension of a garment around the hips, often incorporated in the design of a blouse, jacket or dress.

2 Semi-flared skirts

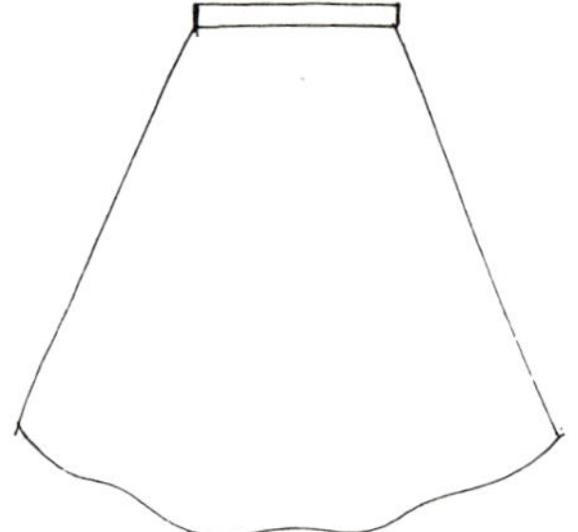

3 Draped skirts

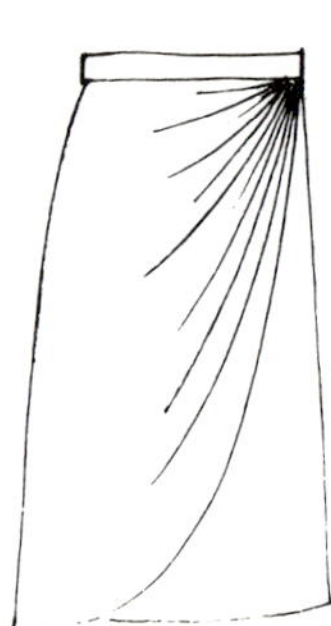

1 Panel skirt

2 Panel skirt with extra flare

3 Full-flared skirt

Design brief

Design a development sheet of summer evening dresses suitable for a summer holiday. Select a fabric, considering the climate in which it would be worn.

The six dresses should be based on a theme using gathers, shirring or flounces as a decorative feature.

Occasion – Evening wear suitable for a party and dancing
Age – 17
Decorative Theme – Gathers, shirring, flounces
Fabric and Colour – Own choice considering the climate and occasion in which it would be worn

Attach sample fabrics to the sheet, adding notes and detail drawings when necessary.

On the right is a design sheet which has been developed based on a collection of summer evening dresses for an older age group. Note the theme of the designs which have been developed using gathers and a draw-string effect at the neck or waist. When producing this type of sheet the designer would add notes, fabrics, and detail drawings. Experiment with papers of texture and colour, working with different media.

Yokes

The yoke may be used on the bodice, waist or skirt. It can be designed in a variety of shapes with contrasting materials and colours.

Often it is used to incorporate fit when cutting the pattern. The effects of the yoke on the shoulder, bodice, waist or hips are constantly used in fashion, from casual sportswear to coats, suits and evening wear.

Yoke shapes featuring surface treatment making the yoke the focal point of a design

The one basic shape has been designed with a variation of yoke shapes. Note the use of yokes on the skirts and the way in which the shape is balanced with the yoke on the bodice.

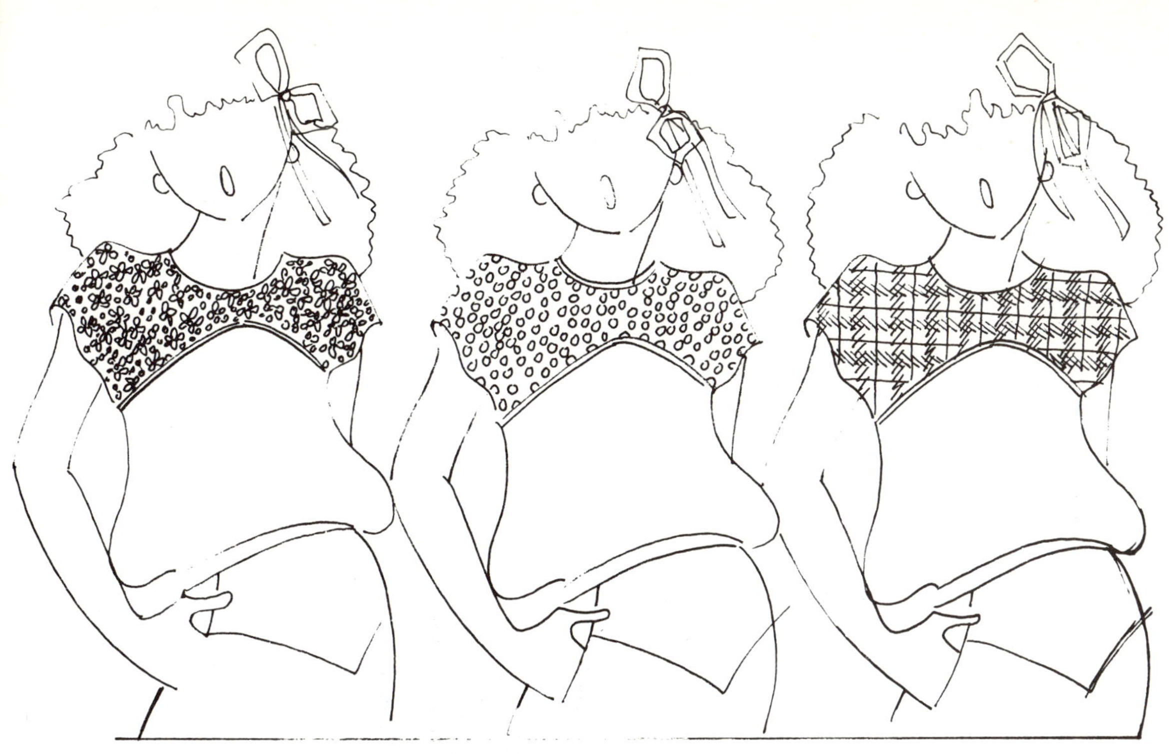

The same shapes used with contrasting fabrics.
Note how different fabrics will give one basic shape a variety of effects.

Yokes featured in a collection of young teenage co-ordinated garments of skirts, blouses and jackets. Note the use of the yoke as introduced at the waist, hips and shoulders, using surface treatment of shirring, smocking and quilting.

Design a collection of six blouses and skirts introducing yokes as a design feature.

Age – Teenage group 14 – 18 years
Occasion – Summer day wear
Fabric – Select suitable fabrics, considering the colour, pattern and weight.
Design Feature – Yokes with surface interest (smocking, shirring or pin tucks).

Research Use colour and pattern as your source of inspiration. Collect fabric samples, relating the colours and patterns. If you have some experience in dress-making, make a selection of samples of different surface effects, e.g. pin tucks, smocking and shirring, from your selected fabrics before producing a design sheet.

Note how the pattern of the fabric changes when you apply the surface treatment to the fabric.

1 Top stitching
2 Shirring
3 Smocking
4 Pin tucks
5 Inset lace trimming and ribbons

Fasteners

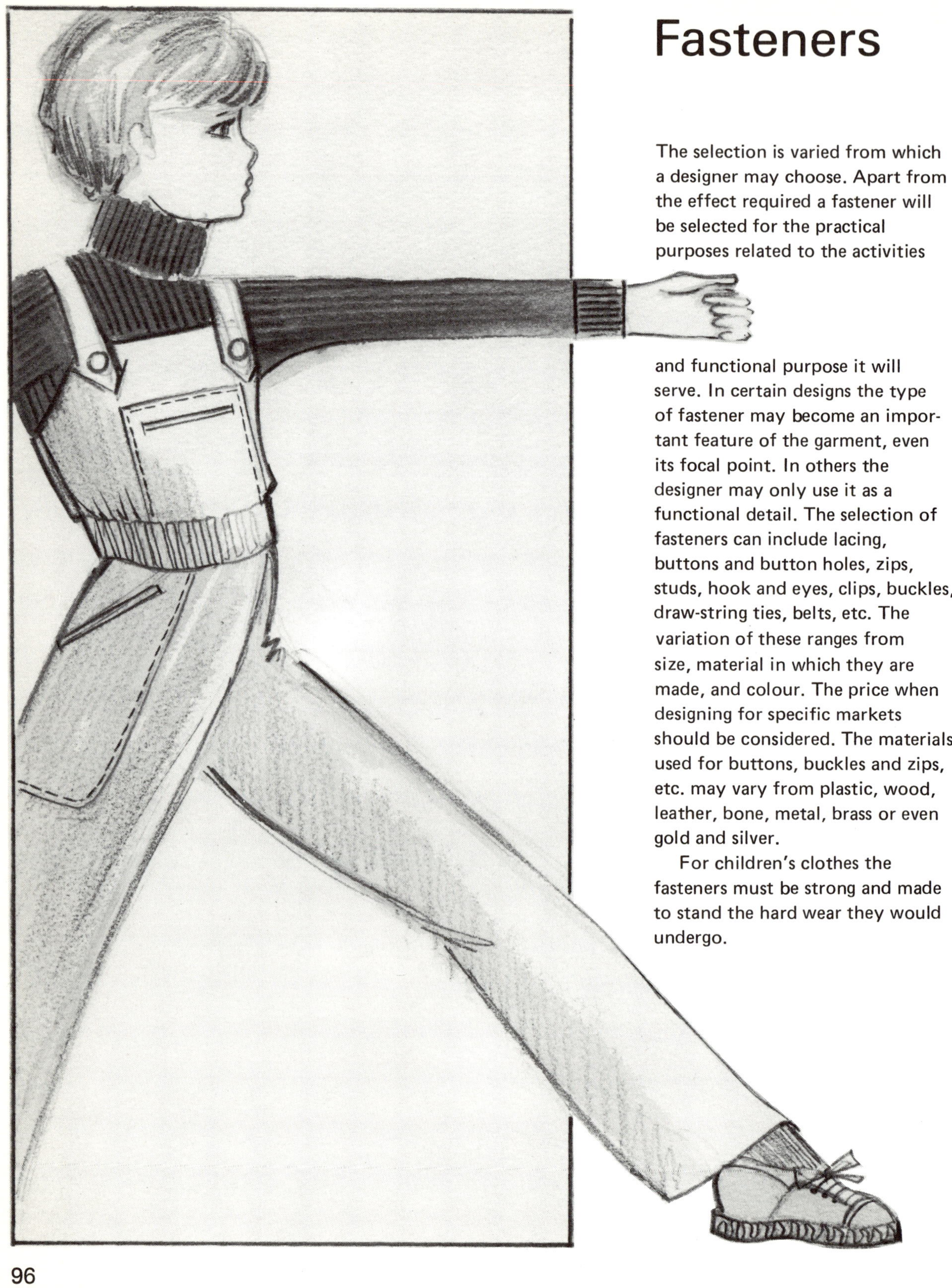

The selection is varied from which a designer may choose. Apart from the effect required a fastener will be selected for the practical purposes related to the activities and functional purpose it will serve. In certain designs the type of fastener may become an important feature of the garment, even its focal point. In others the designer may only use it as a functional detail. The selection of fasteners can include lacing, buttons and button holes, zips, studs, hook and eyes, clips, buckles, draw-string ties, belts, etc. The variation of these ranges from size, material in which they are made, and colour. The price when designing for specific markets should be considered. The materials used for buttons, buckles and zips, etc. may vary from plastic, wood, leather, bone, metal, brass or even gold and silver.

For children's clothes the fasteners must be strong and made to stand the hard wear they would undergo.

Zip Fasteners have become a fashion feature. For children's garments they are very suitable, giving easy access to pockets and openings generally. They are made very strong and will stand up to the hard wear that will be involved. Many variations of length and size are produced in a variety of colours.

Buttons The range available is wide. The styles vary from simple basic designs to attractive decorative designs that would become a design feature on a garment. Buttons may be made from plastic, wood, metal, or may be self-covered. Many pleasing effects may be achieved with the placement of the button on a garment.

Rouleau-Fastenings A very decorative fastening made from a roll or fold of fabric, used for piping and making loops for fastening, but not suitable for a very young age group as it is not very adaptable and would not stand the hard wear of a child's activities.

Tie Fastenings This type of fastening is attractive used as a decorative feature. The ties may be made of cord, ribbons, rouleaus or leather.

Above

Note the use of different fasteners used on the same design giving different effects.

Buttons and button holes

There are many alternatives available to the designer, from a simple shape made from plastic to elaborate designs in wood or metal. In certain instances a designer may create buttons or fasteners made specially; this would, however, add considerably to the costing.

The designs range from modern shapes to copies of antique buttons from different historical periods of fashion.

When selecting consider carefully the size, shape, texture and colour related to the design and the fabric on which it will be placed.

Many designers use buttons purely as a decorative feature on a garment, arranging them in different ways. Experiment with buttons and shapes by placing them on different fabrics against a selection of colours, patterns and textures and note the many different effects achieved.

When designing for a very young age group it would be necessary to consider the safety aspect of the use of buttons, as young children are inclined to remove and put them in the mouth, treating them as sweets.

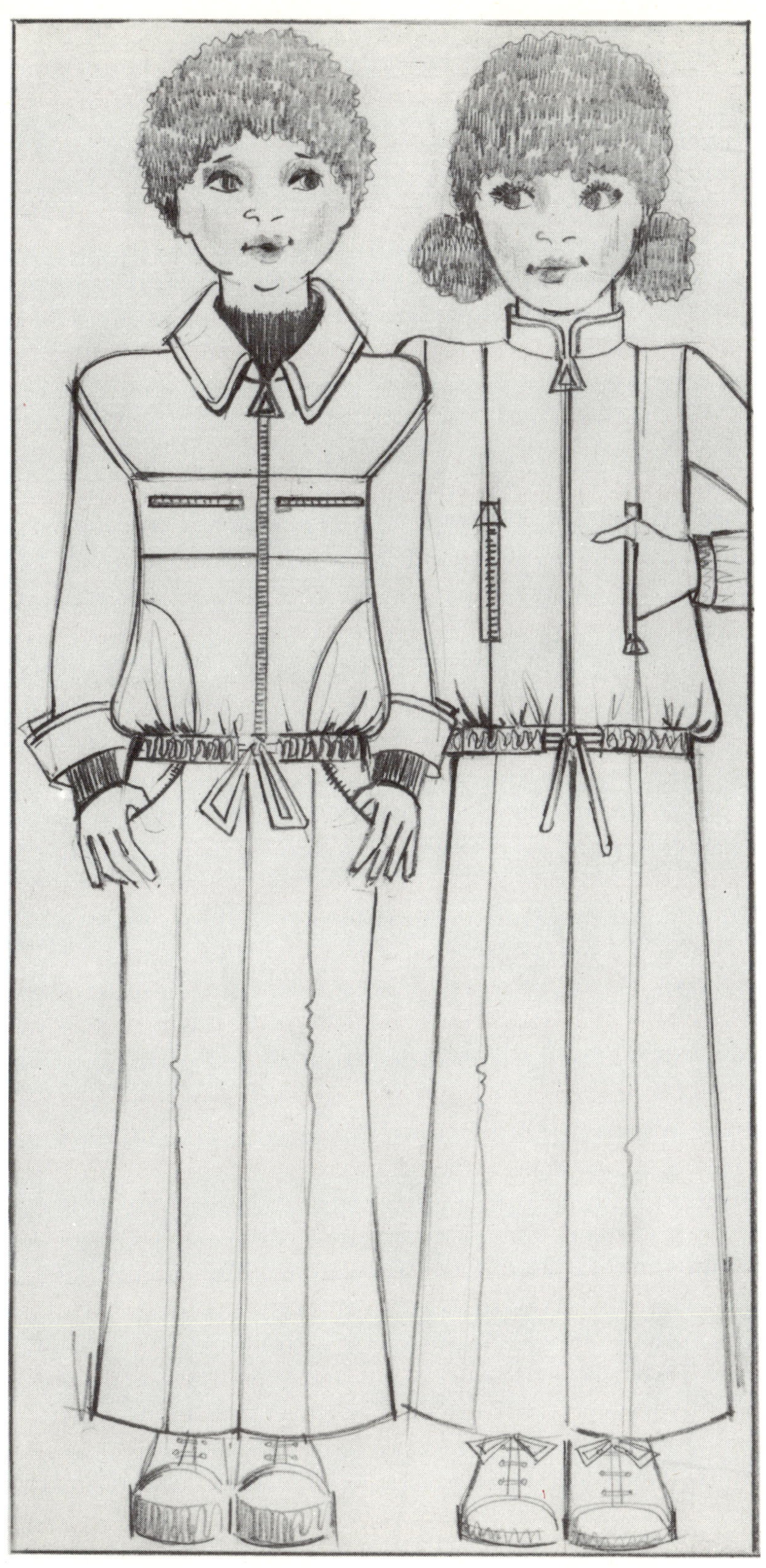

Draw-string

A draw-string or casing is a design feature which has many variations. It can be used decoratively with belts of various widths. This type of fastener may be used at the neck, wrist or waist of a garment.

Design brief

Autumn Season: Casual Play Clothes for Girls and Boys

An exercise considering the design and practical aspects of designing for a specific purpose.

Produce a design development sheet of ideas based on a theme for a collection of children's garments to be worn in a playground out of doors.

The activities would vary from playing on swings, slides, see-saws, roundabouts and climbing. Study the play situations, note the areas of wear and stress and the different movements which may cause strain on seams, etc.

Consider the following aspects when designing:

Age Group – 5 to 12 years.

Fabric – The fabric should be hard wearing, easy to maintain, comfortable and warm to wear.

A selection of button and button hole fasteners:

1 Single Breasted
2 Double Breasted
3 Centre Front Fastener
4 Centre Front Fastener

Right **Braces**
A very practical as well as a good design feature on casual garments for children. They are made in different materials and colours with decorative patterns. The sizes and widths vary.

Straps and buckles
Straps and buckles produce a very secure fastening on pockets and openings. The straps and buckles can be made in different materials.

Snap fastener
Snap fasteners may be obtained in many sizes. They may be used decoratively as well as functionally. They are very suitable for children's wear as they are strong and adaptable.

Fly fastening
With this type of fastening the buttons are completely concealed, giving a neat and clean appearance to a design.

Other fasteners:
Buckles
Chains
Clips
Hook and Eye
Hardwear fasteners
Velcro
Belts of leather, metal, chain, cord, etc.

Observe the ways in which different styles of fasteners have been used in relation to a design and the decorative effects achieved.

Make drawings of the many different types in your sketch book and design variations of your own for reference when designing.

Patchwork
A selected number of shaped pieces of patterned or plain fabric stitched together and used as a regular fabric. An entire garment may be made of patchwork, or patchwork may be used on areas of a design.

A selection of zip fasteners used on the pocket of a garment.

Design Project

Design a collection of co-ordinated casual garments. The collection may consist of trousers, jackets, coats, skirts and jumpers.

Occasion — Casual day wear

Age — 14 to 16 years

Season — Winter

Fabric and colour — own choice. Consider the fashion and the age you are designing for.

Fashion Feature — the fastening on the openings used as a decorative feature (see illustrations).

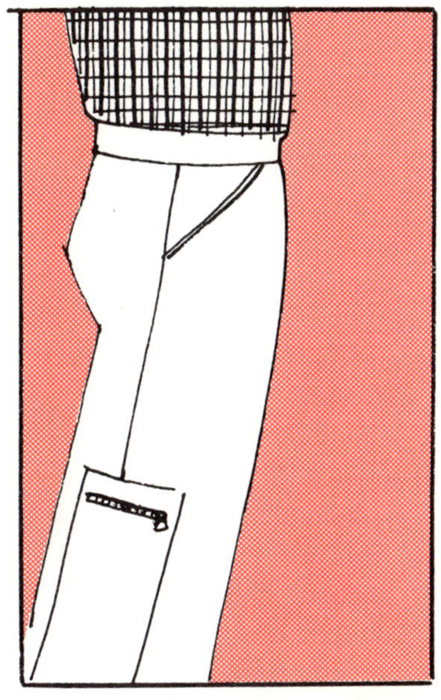

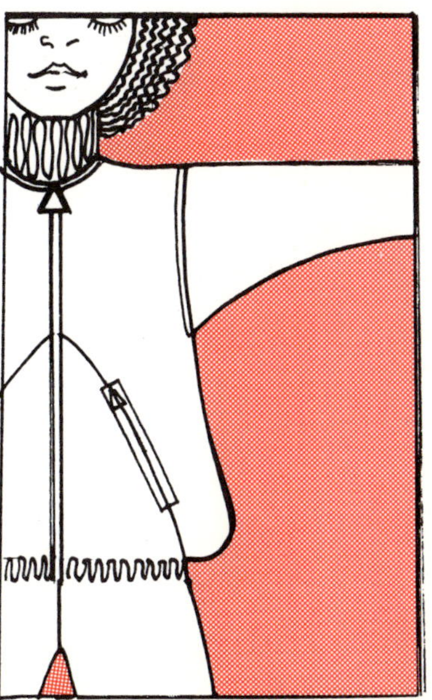

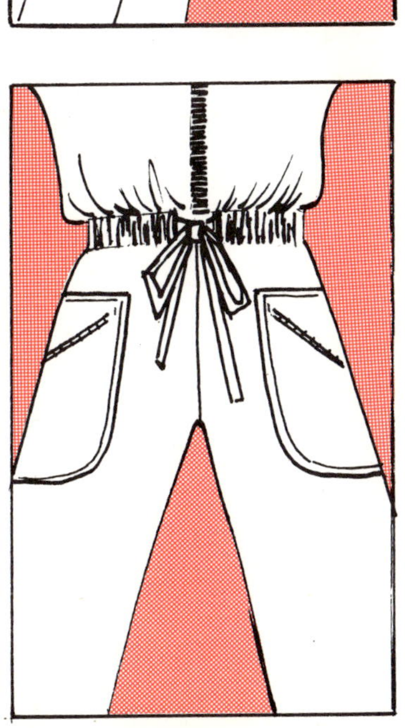

Pockets

Many variations of pocket designs are based on only a few styles. In some garments the pocket will become an important design feature. In other instances it may serve a functional purpose only and would be concealed within the garment.

The basic pocket styles are the patch, slit and pocket with flap.

The use of variations in shape, stitching, piping, fabrics, fastenings, etc. will provide the designer with many ideas and variations.

When producing ideas for a garment where the pocket is to serve a functional role, it is important to have an understanding of the activity, sport or purpose the garment is for and the situation in which it will be worn. The designer must consider carefully the placement, size and fastening of the pocket.

Many style features may be used. On the following pages a number of ideas have been illustrated.

1 Patch pocket – Pocket applied to the surface of a garment. Designed in many shapes, with or without a flap.

2 Welt pocket – The pocket has the effect of a large bound button hole.

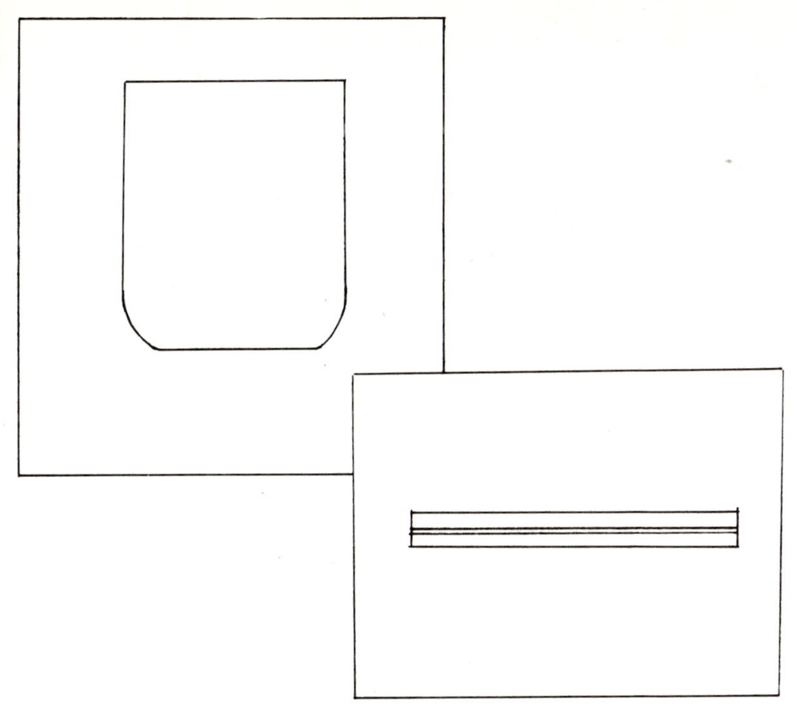

The pocket is constructed on two basic methods. Pockets of self fabric are applied to the garment. The other type are of lining situated on the inside of a garment, with an opening on the outside through a slash or seam, and may be covered by a flap or welt.

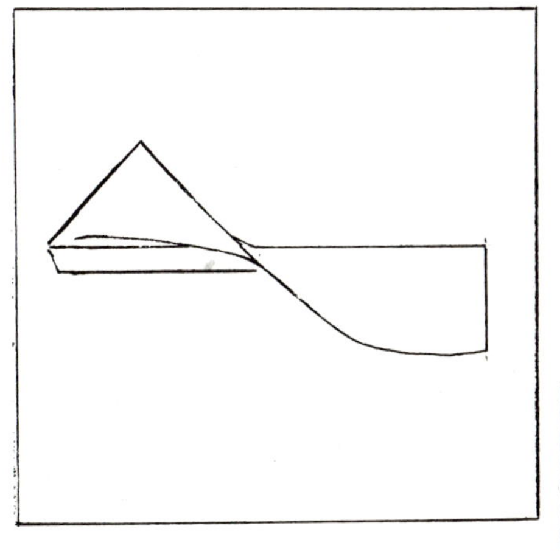

3 Self welt pocket – The flap and welt are combined for a tailored appearance.

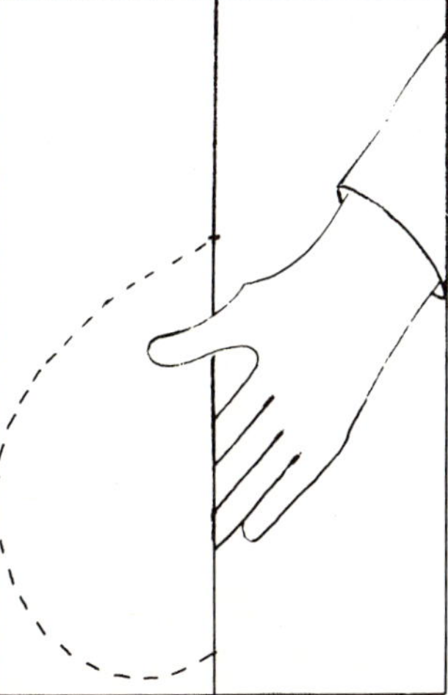

4 Pockets placed in a seam – Concealed pockets are often placed in front or side seams. The seam pocket is often made of lining fabric faced at its edge with the same fabric as the garment.

Pockets placed in a seam.
The raincoat illustrates a welt pocket.

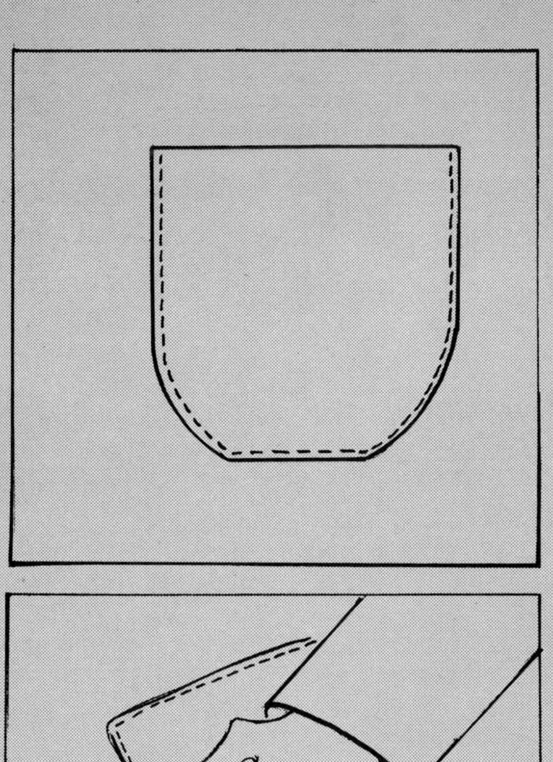

1 Patch Pocket

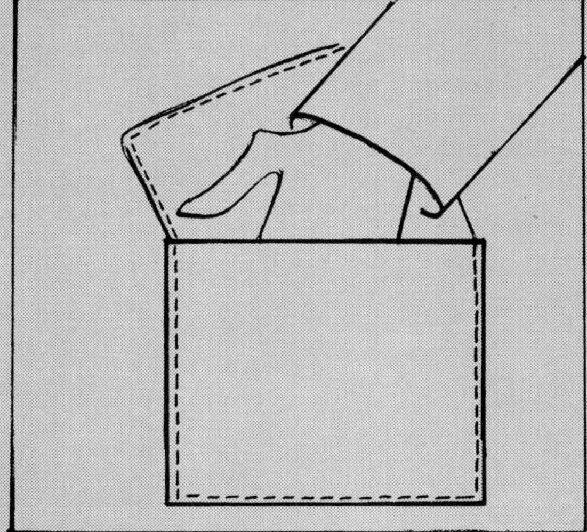

2 Patch Pocket with Flap

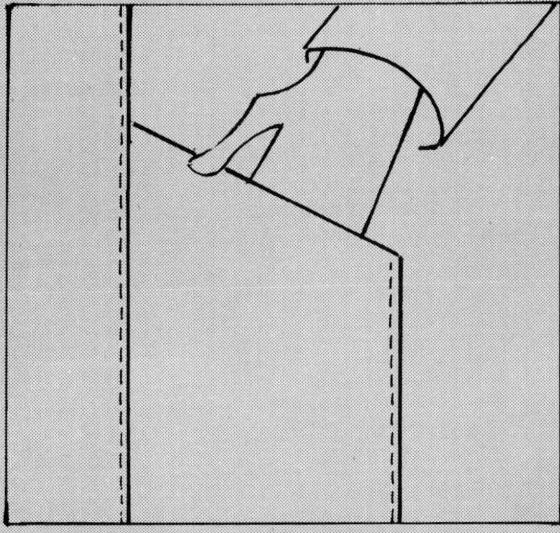

3 Patch Pocket attached to seam

Design project

Produce a design development sheet of six casual garments suitable for the 4 to 6 year age group, based on the dungaree style. Introduce the patch pocket as a functional and style feature within the design. Remember to design the back views and suggest suitable fabrics. Introduce detail sketches on your design sheet.

Age – 4 to 6 years, Girls and Boys
Occasion – Casual Play Garments
Season – Summer
Fabric – Cotton Denim
Fashion Feature – Patch pockets with style interest.
Colour – For safety reasons the colours should be bright, making it easy to observe a child under certain conditions.
Texture, Pattern, Trimmings – The texture, pattern and trimmings may be used for design effect, considering the fabrics that would appeal to a young age group.
Fastenings – should be strong, easy and adaptable to adjust, according to the climate.
Pockets – Placement for easy access and protection against loss.
Collars – Adaptable for weather changes.
Areas of stress and wear – The need of protection reinforcement or replacement.

Patch Pockets with flaps fastened down in different ways.

1 Buckle Strap
2 Button and Button hole
3 Press stud
4 Concealed velcro

Exercise
Make a number of shapes suitable for patch pockets and suggest different features such as pleating, tucks, stitching, piping, different shaped flaps and fastenings. The fastenings may vary from straps, buttons, zips, buckles, press studs, etc.

Trimming and surface effects

Many results may be achieved with the use of trimmings and surface effects. The choice of trimmings designed for garments of all occasions is a wide one. The designer should be careful in selecting the trimmings for a garment, relating the braids, etc. to the fabric on which they will be applied. Trimmings may be used to emphasise the shape of a collar or pocket, to add interest to the hem of a skirt or sleeve. Combined with the colour, texture and pattern of a fabric many pleasing results may be obtained.

By the use of smocking, shirring, pleating and pin tucks, etc. the designer may achieve many effective ideas, altering the surface of the fabric and creating new patterns. These effects may be enhanced further by the use of embroidery and applied decoration.

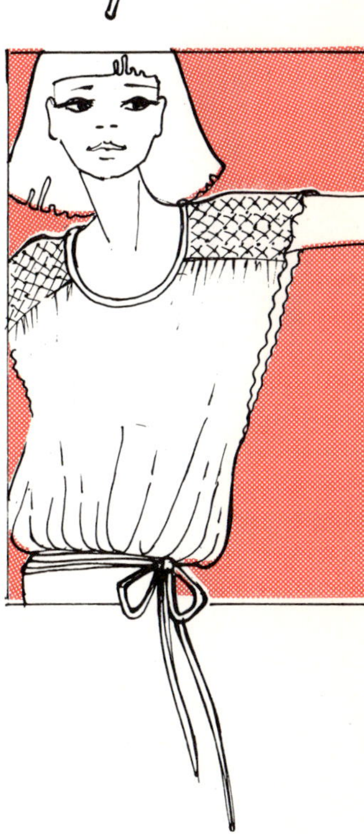

Smocking

Smocking adds surface interest to a fabric and is a design feature for many garments used on a variety of fabrics from velvet, satin, cotton and wool, etc. Certain patterned fabrics look very attractive when smocking has been applied. Smocking is also used to hold fullness in even folds.

Shirring

Shirring is achieved by putting an elastic thread through the material. It may be used single or repeated a number of times.

Piping

May be used set-in to a seam or as a surface decoration. It is made by covering cord with bias fabric.

Rouleau

A strip of material cut on the bias applied folded, with or without a filling. Used as piping applied to a garment in seams. May also be used for decorative features as illustrated.

Rouleau

1 Neck line with rouleau ties with shirring at waist and shoulder yokes
2 Shirring and rouleaus at waist with rouleau straps
3 Shirring rouleaus and gathers at neck line
4 Smocking in shoulder yokes with rouleau tie at waist.

Braids
A large selection of braids are obtainable in many widths, designs and materials. Add sample pieces to your collection. Note how braids have been applied to garment designs generally.

Below
Braids applied to garments, giving a decorative design effect

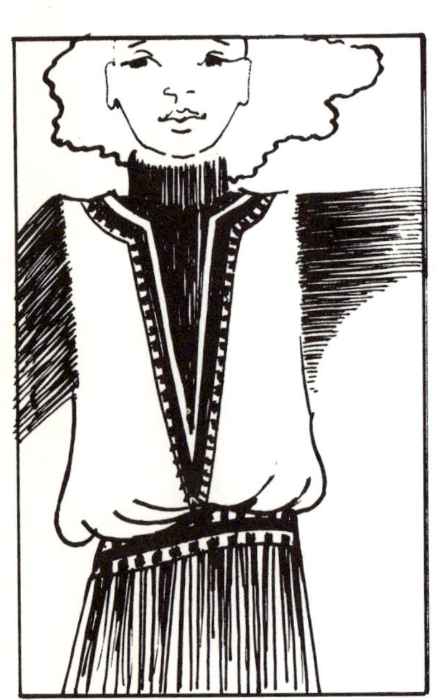

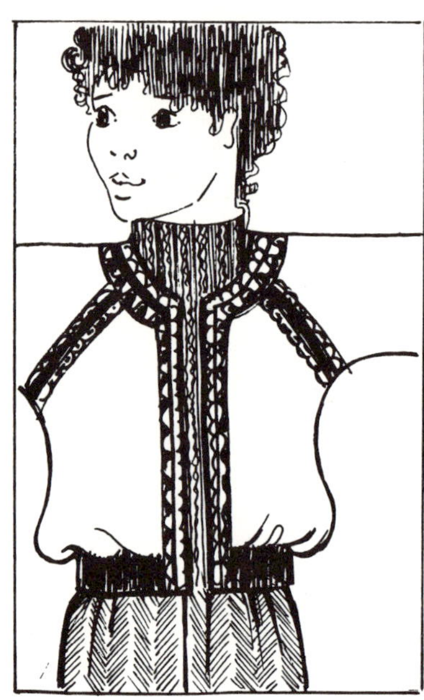

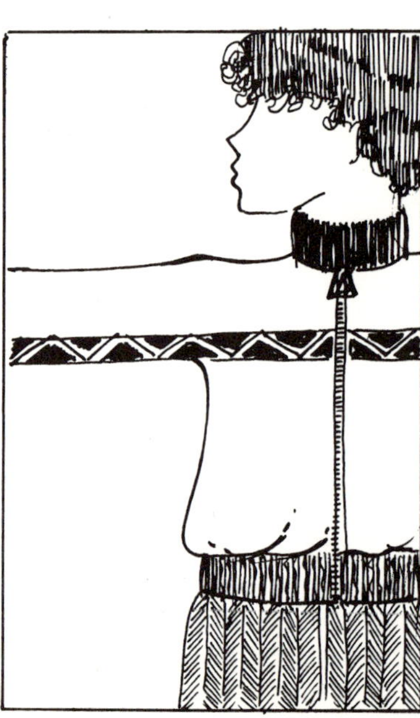

Design Project

Beach wear. Design a collection of six beach dresses or separates incorporating in the designs rouleau ties, straps or trimmings as a feature. Select fabrics suitable for a summer dress considering those which are easy to pack and maintain (i.e. drip-dry, non-crease, lightweight and cool).

Occasion — Holiday beach wear

Climate — Very warm, summer season

Fabric — own choice. Consider colour, pattern, texture and weight.

Fashion Image — Elegantly casual for a teenage market, 16-20 years.

Produce a collection of designs as a design development sheet of casual garments for a young age group from five to 12 years. The garments should be suitable for playing in and should introduce top stitching as a decorative feature. Consider the fabric you select and the colour combined with a knitted jumper, if the design requires it. Design a suitable hat to create a total effect.

Age Group – 5 to 12 years
Occasion – Play situation
Fabric and colour – blue denim – or own choice
Trimming – Top stitching in contrasting colour
Accessorise with hats and jumpers.

The design sheet on the right develops the theme of pocket interest, experimenting with the many variations of the patch pockets on a collection of casual garments based on the cut of dungarees. The sketches have been produced with a Rotring pen on a sheet of layout paper, then flat mounted on a sheet of light-weight card.

Quilting

Quilting is achieved by stitching through two or more layers of fabric. A layer of light padding, cotton, wadding or foam rubber is added. Matching or contrasting threads may be used.

Pre-quilted fabrics may also be purchased ready-made.

Quilting may be used on the design of a garment with pleasing results. Apart from its decorative effect the quilting will add extra warmth to a fabric. It may be used on the collar of a jacket or on the hem of a skirt, sleeve or coat. The entire garment may be quilted in some designs. The effect may be used in different ways: to define the shape of a yoke, for a collar, pocket or as a decorative motive.

Trapanto quilting

Quilting in which the background is left unpadded and only the design stands out in relief.

1 Quilted Bolero

2 Quilted Shawl-collar and tie belt

3 Quilted straps and pockets

4 Quilted yoke and cuff

Design Project

Design a collection of dresses with a co-ordinated jacket or bolero suitable for day wear. Introduce quilting in different areas of the garments as a decorative theme.

If you are able to sew it is an advantage, before designing, to select sample lengths of fabric and to experiment with different methods of quilting, observing the effects achieved when the fabric is quilted.

Occasion — Day wear
Age — 12 — 14 years
Fabric and Colour — Own choice (select a variety of samples based on a colour scheme and create a story board before starting on the design sheet).
Surface Treatment — Quilting — experiment with samples creating different effects. Study the effects of quilting used on garments generally.
Source of Inspiration — Study periods of national costume in museums and costume books for inspiration in the use of fabric and colour.

Presenting design work

Presentation

It is important when preparing work for an assessment, examination, competition or interview to present your work so as to complement the designs, to give the right impression and make it a pleasure for the interviewer or examiner to view your work.

Assessment and examinations

The work for an examination is usually prepared according to the requirements of the examination board. Often internal assessments are made of the students' work and presented within a display area. The work displayed usually includes, depending on the course, design sheets, presentation drawings, sketch books, areas of research and examples of other aspects of the course, which could include embroidery, knitting, accessories and samples of surface decoration. Some examples of garments, fabric printing designed and made would be shown, together with patterns, grading charts and costing sheets.

Display

When displaying work for exhibition it is effective to use a single colour scheme throughout the display, taking into account the background of the screens and related to the colour of the mounting card and work. It is important to indicate the type of lettering which may be used and to be specific when giving information when required about work displayed.

Other work not displayed on the screen should be shown in a portfolio with the work mounted on a lightweight card all of the same size. When work is being assessed or on general display it will require some protection. Large transparent folders are very effective in protecting work.

Garments may be displayed in different ways according to the availability of stands, etc. A dress stand is a good way of showing a garment. Should one not be available, it can be effective to display the garment on a hanger against the screen. In certain instances the design may not be suitable. Should you pin a garment to a screen take care not to distort your design.

Make it as easy as possible for an examiner to inspect the way in which garments have been made. Do not use too many pins, effective as they can be in a display; they often give a falsifying effect to the original design — apart from causing complications when the work has to be removed when examined.

Presentation and mounting

Mounting cards can be obtained in a wide variety of thicknesses, colours and textures.

Consider with care the colour and texture of the card related to your work and which one would be the most effective complement.

Heavy card can be of considerable weight when you have a collection of work to carry. For interviews it is advisable to select a thin card which is light and easy to carry. The size will be determined by the work. It is, however, advisable to produce drawings which are not going to be difficult to handle. A good size is A.3.

Select card and make the cutting line with a pencil. Take care to measure the window so as to overlap the drawing.

Use a sharp cutting knife and score the line with the aid of a steel rule.

Fix the drawing from the back with selotape.

Interviews

When taking your work for an interview it is advisable to mount the selected design sheets, photographs and presentation work to a standard size, preferably on a light-weight card neatly packed in a portfolio. It is customary to write your name and also to date each piece of work on the back, and to add any specific information related to the work.

Window Mounting
Window cut-out of card with work mounted from the back.

Flat Mounting
Work placed on card fixed with a good adhesive spray or gum.

Transparent Folder
Transparent envelope for displaying work enabling you to display work from both sides.

List of art materials

Fashion boards High quality board extra thick will take charcoal, crayon, gouache, tempera and water colour paints.
Water colour boards Saunders Water Colour Boards prepared from a mould-made paper. The paper has an even surface.
Bristol board The board has a high rag content with a fine white surface. Ideal for pen and ink work.
Pasteboard An inexpensive white board for paste-up and general studio use.
Illustration boards A board with a smooth surface which will take ink, crayon, pencil, wash or colour. Produced in different sizes.
Cartridge paper White paper with a finely grained surface suitable for pencil, crayon and colour. This paper is made in different thicknesses and qualities.
Coloured cartridge paper The surface has a slight texture. Suitable for colour work. Will take water colour and pastels.
Layout pads White layout detail paper with a surface ideal for ink and pencil. Available in different sizes.
Ingres paper The surface of this paper is ideal for pastel and tempera work. Good selection of colours.
Coloured tissue papers Unglazed tissue paper, available in a large range of colours, is used in studios to produce inexpensive colour effects. The paper can be stuck to board or paper surfaces with Cow gum or adhesive spray.
Tracing paper and pads Obtainable in sheets of different sizes or pads.
Herculene tracing film Polyester film of good quality. Will take pencil and ink, ideal for photocopying and also colour separation work. May also be used for the protection of work.
Permatrace Film with excellent drawing surface for ink and pencil. This film is virtually indestructible.
Tracing cloth Good quality tracing cloth for work that must withstand considerable handling and wear.
Detail paper A white paper with a high degree of transparency. Suitable when working from original roughs.

Pencils
A large selection of pencils is obtainable; the type of pencil used would depend on the effect required.
Pencils (wood cased) The degree of hardness is printed on each pencil:
6B is very soft, 9H very hard
F and HB are medium
EX is extremely soft.
Stabilo pencils This pencil will write on any surface: film, glossy photographs, metals, etc.
Charcoal pencils Gives the same effect as pure charcoal sticks. Made in hard, medium or soft qualities.
Carbon pencils This pencil will produce a dull matt finish.
Black pencils Heavy extra large leads for bold drawings in matt jet black.
Coloured pencils A large variety of makes is available with a good range of colours.
Chinagraph (wax based) This pencil is impervious to water and dampness, but it is possible to remove with a dry cloth.

Pens
A large selection of pens is available; listed are some chosen for the different effects that may be achieved.
Rapidograph pens Technical pens that provide a means of drawing without the need of constant refilling. The drawing point may be replaced with different sizes. Many pleasing effects may be obtained with the use of this pen, and also in combination with others.
Osmiroid fountain pens A pen for lettering and script writing. A large range of interchangeable screw-in nibs (not suitable with Indian ink).
Technos drawing pen The Pelikan Technos is a cartridge-filled drawing pen. Pen points are designed for different jobs, e.g. ruling, stencilling, and free hand. Many interchangeable points are available.
Osmiroid Sketch fountain pen A very versatile sketching pen which provides a wide variety of line thickness from bold to a fine outline. This pen is fitted with a reservoir to maintain a constant ink flow. Indian ink should not be used.
Pen holders Many very simple wood or plastic pen holders with nibs are obtainable at a small cost.

A large selection of paints of varying qualities are manufactured:
Watercolours
Designer Colours
Poster Paints
Tubes of Oil Paint.
Pastels Pastels vary depending on the quality.
Coloured inks A large selection of coloured inks are available, some of which are waterproof.

Brushes Brushes are made in many sizes and qualities (sable, hog and squirrel hair).
Transparent acetate sheet Cellulose acetate film. Suitable for covering art work and presentation.
Presentation books Fitted with clear acetate pockets, ideal for presentation of work – photographs, drawings, etc.
Portfolios Strong durable portfolios in different sizes for storing art work.
Leathercloth portfolios Ideal for the protection of art work and carrying. Fitted with handle, two fasteners and a centre lock and key. Made in different sizes.
Stanley knife A craft knife with replaceable blades, ideal for cutting thick paper, heavy card, plastics, etc.
Swivel-head knives Cuts irregular curves, may be locked for straight lines.
Double-sided adhesive tape Suitable for quick-mounting. Adhesive on both sides.
Protective sprays Spray to protect art work against damage – obtainable in gloss or matt.
Adhesive in aerosol cans Spray adhesive – colourless and water repellent. Will stick cloth, board, paper.
Cow gum Transparent rubber solution suitable for pasting work up. Sold in tins or tubes.
Copydex Very strong latex adhesive, may be used with paper and fabric.
Gum eraser or paper cleaner A soft pliable eraser gum. Suitable for cleaning art work. Will not damage the surface of the paper.
Kneaded eraser A putty rubber that can be moulded to the shape required.
Staedtler Mars plastic For use on drafting film, tracing cloth or paper.
Soft eraser A white soft eraser for soft lead.
Masking tape Tape seals with light pressure, with a water-repellent back.
Drafting tape Designed to hold film or paper to a drawing board and removed without damage. A very thin, adhesive crepe paper tape.
Light box A box with a glass top containing a light, used for tracing.
Transpaseal Flexible sheet of thin transparent plastic coated with a pressure-sensitive adhesive, obtainable in clear gloss or matt finish. Suitable for covering art work.
Air brush The air brush provides perfectly even tones, graded tints and soft lines, also the blending of colours. Operated by a motor compressor or compressed air propellant aerosols.